PROCESS AND PRACTICE
IN FAMILY THERAPY

SECOND EDITION

PROCESS AND PRACTICE
IN FAMILY THERAPY

SECOND EDITION

GERALD H. ZUK, Ph.D.
Zuk Institute of Family Therapy and
Beck Psychiatric Medical Group
Los Angeles County
California

HUMAN SCIENCES PRESS, INC.
72 FIFTH AVENUE
NEW YORK, N.Y. 10011-8004

For mother, now gone; and for Carmencita

Printed in the United States of America
987654321

Library of Congress Cataloging in Publication Data

Zuk, Gerald H.
  Process and practice in family therapy.

  Includes index.
  1. Family psychotherapy. I. Title.
RC488.5.Z83   1986   616.89'15   86-7154
ISBN 0-89885-276-5

CONTENTS

PREFACE TO THE SECOND EDITION

My work has been a progression of interlocking themes developed in family therapy practice. The first theme was pathogenic relating, formulated initially in the early 1960s in papers exploring the meaning of laughter and silencing. I returned to this theme much later, in the early 1980s, when I defined certain "styles of relating" and blaming as, together with silencing, the three commonest forms of pathogenic relating encountered in family therapy.

The second theme, Go-Between Process, which is a role-related theory of doing family therapy, was formulated in the middle and late 1960s, but then in the mid-1970s I added a third role, the celebrant, to the two that I had initially defined (the go-between and side-taker), and described the interrelation of the three roles as comprising Go-Between Process conducted by the family therapist.

The third theme began to occupy my thinking in the early 1970s—the problem of engaging families in therapy, and families' readiness for therapy, because these were interconnected problems. In the '70s it became evident to me that most therapists were paying mere lip service to what they had been experiencing clinically, and must have been observing there: that in outpatient clinics, many families were not especially motivated for therapy, the number of premature dropouts was large, and that most families imposed limits on the time the therapist could work with them. I felt it was necessary to bring the themes of engagement and readiness for therapy strongly to the attention of colleagues, and stressed that these were the most serious practical problems in the field and impeding its progress.

In various papers in the early '70s I spelled out an engagement process aimed at capitalizing on a family's readiness to undertake the stress of therapy, and factors in families' backgrounds that enhanced or limited their readiness for therapy—factors such as social class, religion, race, and various crises that affected most families but were relatively unpredictable (such as job loss, divorce, physical illness).

The theme that occupied me during the late '70s was founded in a discovery that most family conflict could be defined in terms of a conflict of *values*, and that commonly two sets of values were involved—and these I entitled the continuity and discontinuity sets. I was somewhat surprised that it was possible, within limits, to predict which partner in a marital conflict would espouse continuity values, and which discontinuity, but I was more surprised to find that these value sets also discriminated conflict between parents and their children with regularity, and also discriminated conflict between the family and community with regularity.

In the early '80s I became concerned with the theme of the truncated nuclear family, which was based on the prior formulation of continuity and discontinuity values, and described a condition when these values became markedly polarized. When such a polarization occurred, the potential for pathogenic relating was greatly increased. Offspring tended to ally with their mothers against their fathers, and with continuity values against discontinuity values because in the nuclear unit the mother is the primary exponent of continuity values, the father of discontinuity values. As the offspring moved through adolescence and into young adulthood, they experienced difficulty with agencies and institutions outside the family because those agencies and institutions represented discontinuity values. Some of the offspring became disturbed because of their alienation from discontinuity values.

When the first edition of this book appeared in 1975, one critic described it as "too conservative." I believe the critic was referring to my disinclination to use certain elements of showmanship in my therapy, mainly because families, which are essentially conservative, are made anxious by showmanship; and perhaps because my claims for outcome were—certainly in contrast to other claimants at the time—conservative. I do not think differently today. What was judged too conservative in 1975 may be deemed different today.

Another critic claimed that the earlier edition had overtones of bias, especially class, race, and sex bias. I imagine that critic was referring to my insistence on describing what most experienced colleagues were well aware of but were oddly shy to address in writing: that families differed greatly in their readiness for therapy, and that factors such as class and race, among numerous other factors, influenced readiness. It may be that I did not present my observations in the most palatable fashion, but I thought it would be unethical not to present them, despite my awareness that there is, in some mental health professionals, a wish to equate and integrate certain of the ideals of a democratic society with the "truths" of clinical practice, even in the face of obvious discrepancies.

It may not be pleasant to recognize that all families exhibit prejudice and bias—even those that have themselves been victims—and that the most immediate goals of family therapy are not to eliminate prejudice and bias. It is wise for the therapist to recognize the various forms of hatefulness in families, as in individuals, and to learn the means to manage the hatefulness so that it does not prevent progress in therapy. More than one likes to think, prejudice and bias are common among therapists, and most dangerous when denied or converted into an ideology or "cause."

Despite these criticisms of the first edition, it gained an audience and eventually was recognized as a leading text in the field.

This second edition redresses what may have been an imbalance in the earlier in favor of transcript material at the expense of the more finely honed clinical essay. Five clinical essays have been added, all of which originally appeared in the *International Journal of Family Therapy*, and I wish to thank Human Sciences Press of New York for permission to include the material here.

The five essays are added to Part I, "Concepts and Classifications." Chapter 3 of Part I is from the Spring 1981 issue of *IJFT*, and describes a new form of pathogenic relating which is titled "style of relating." Chapter 6 of Part I, from the Fall 1984 issue of *IJFT*, describes another form of pathogenic relating — blaming. These chapters are further elaborations of the theme of pathogenic relating, which I began to explore in the early 1960s with studies of silencing in family interviews.

Chapter 4 of Part I, from the Spring 1982 issue of *IJFT*, and Chapter 7 of Part I, from the Spring 1985 issue, are elaborations of the truncated nuclear family theme. Chapter 4 is an analysis of the film *Ordinary People* from the perspective of the truncated nuclear family concept. Chapter 7 attempts to relate changes in the social structure of American society in particular that have contributed to the emergence of the truncated nuclear family as the garden-variety form of family psychopathology seen by clinicians today (Zuk, 1985).

I think it is not useful to use psychiatric terminology to "diagnose" families — the truncated nuclear family is not a psychiatric diagnosis. The efforts by family researchers to differentiate families according to certain criteria have not proved of much use to clinicians, but I think the truncated nuclear family concept is useful for clinicians working with troubled families.

Chapter 5 of Part I, from the Fall 1983 issue of *IJFT*, analyzes clinical depression from the perspective of value theory. It proposes that depression is a resultant of value "diffusion" — the splitting apart of the continuity and discontinuity values that comprise an essential component of individual personality, just as they can be said to comprise an essential component of "family personality."

A new Chapter 4 is added to Part III of this edition, which is from the Fall 1982 issue of *IJFT*. The chapter is an exchange between myself and several Argentine mental health experts representing different theoretical viewpoints regarding the case, entitled "Runaway Wife", presented in Chapters 2 and 3 of Part III.

This edition, as well as the earlier, is intended for the mental health clinician who works primarily with families and couples, but it contains material that

should be of some interest to all mental health workers. Names and other iden-
tifying information in cases reported have been fictionalized throughout the
text.

GERALD H. ZUK

PREFACE TO THE FIRST EDITION

This book is intended to train family therapists, and to inform psychotherapists and other mental health practitioners about family functioning, because the family is a social unit of such relevance for their work.

Part I, "Concepts and Classifications," consists of two chapters that extend what I began in a prior book, *Family Therapy: A Triadic-based Approach* (Behavioral Publications, 1972). In chapter 6 of that book I took the position that a factor underlying psychiatric and/or conduct disturbances of all kinds in children and adolescents was an increasingly mother-dominant nuclear family. In this type of family the values expressed by mothers predominate, and these values differ from those expressed by their husbands. There are differences in the value orientations of men and women—husbands and wives—and these differences can generate a variety of forms of pathogenic relating in which children can be scapegoated. Because emotionally children are more loyal to their mothers than their fathers, they are prone to adopt their mothers' values. Because fathers in American families are so frequently absent or peripheral, children are estranged from the values that reflect their fathers' thinking and attitudes. As the children pass into adolescence and young adulthood, they come in contact with the society at large—which is predicated mainly on the values of their fathers, that is, male values. The conflict is inevitable, and the result can be devastating to both the child and society.

In the latter section of Chapter 2 in Part I, I attempt a discrimination of values espoused by men (fathers) and women (mothers). I use the term discontinuity to refer to those values more characteristic of males (fathers), and the term continuity to stand for those values more characteristic of women (mothers). But discontinuity and continuity also discriminate values espoused by the older generation as compared to the younger. And I note also that the family reflects more the *continuity* values than do other institutions, which mainly reflect the *discontinuity* values. The implications of these differences for family therapy are explored.

At the beginning of Chapter 2 of Part I is a development of my notion of pathogenic relating in families; specifically, how the family therapist determines its presence. Although symptoms and history play a role in its determination, fundamentally it is a formulation by the therapist of what he has observed directly in interviews and which he himself may have helped produce, for the therapist sometimes must evoke pathogenic relating when the family seeks to hide its presence from him.

About at the middle of Chapter 2, I introduce the concept of the therapist as celebrant. This is a third role which contrasts with the two that I have described in previous publications: the go-between and side-taker, which are fundamental positions taken by the therapist in conducting go-between process. The short-term nature of most family therapy requires that attention be paid to the therapist's role as celebrant; that is, as one who, like a priest or minister, or lawyer or physician, or policeman or civic official, is empowered to affirm or deny that a change has occurred or is about to occur in the family. Sometimes the family therapist is fixed in a role similar to one of those institutional figures referred to above (priest or minister, etc.). It can be a powerful therapeutic role even if it is typically exercised for only a brief period. In American society the therapist is taking on more than in the past the mantle of the celebrant. He is more and more present at special transitions which are occurring in persons or couples and families; he is more and more present at critical junctures in people's lives.

In Chapter 1 of Part I is a classification of various kinds of family therapy: the crisis-oriented type, the short-term type, the middle-range type, and the long-term type. The goal of each varies somewhat. Experience has shown that even relatively intact families will limit the amount of time the therapist will have access, so a technique for engagement of families must be cultivated with this fact in mind. Chapter 1 describes my technique for engaging families which utilizes an evaluation series of three or four interviews to encourage continuation. The first goal of the therapist is to engage the family; the second is to assess the picture of pathogenic relating.

Chapter 1 also describes why I think the division of family therapy into a traditional format of beginning, middle and termination phases is neither accurate nor fruitful. My experience suggests an engagement phase followed by a series of engagements on issues or events that are of interest to the family or the therapist. Termination occurs when either the therapist or family decides not to engage on the new issue or event. Family therapy really consists of a series of what might be called critical incidents beginning with the actual engagement of the family (i.e. its willingness to continue with the therapist beyond the evaluation period, and the therapist's *acceptance* of the family beyond the evaluation), continuing on with various engagements on issues or events, each of which raises tensions, and ending with a termination brought about when family or therapist decides not to engage on a new issue or event. The termination can be due to an improvement in the problem which the family presented, which has lowered tensions; or it can be due to the introduction of an issue which the family is not prepared to deal with, which has raised tensions.

Part II is entitled "Diagnosis, Technique and Change," and consists of two hour-long conversations held on successive Wednesdays in August, 1973, with several psychiatric residents from the Eastern Pennsylvania Psychiatric Institute in their 2nd and 3rd years of the residency. The residents, most just beginning to carry their first cases in family therapy, sought my response to a wide range of items—from my attitude toward specific techniques used in family therapy, to my philosophy of therapeutic change.

In Part II, I touch upon, in the unique format of the residents' interrogatory, a number of points made in the chapters comprising Part I: on pathogenic relating; on the functions of the therapist conducting go-between process, with special reference to his role as a celebrant; on engagement and termination; on the various types of family therapy as determined by the length of contact with the family; on the goals of therapy as related to the types; and on the sets of values expressed in interviews by families.

Somewhat mischievously, the residents raise a number of questions regarding techniques toward which I suspect they knew I held negative attitudes; for example, cotherapy, videotape playback, simulated families, and certain other training devices used in family therapy. I try to explain my opposition to these devices, but also conditions under which they might be useful.

There is a discussion in Part II of the readiness of families for therapy—particularly the impact of social class, ethnic, racial and religious factors on readiness. One of the major limitations families impose is the distrust that many have of language and/or words. Psychotherapy is a process carried out mainly in the context of an exchange of words, of language; words and language are its main currency. Many poor minority families have a distrust of words and those who use them well, as therapists are supposed to be able to do. The distrust imposes a basic limitation on family therapy as well as other kinds.

Particularly in the case of poor minority families, the sex, age, race and religious background of the *therapist* are factors that affect their responsiveness to the process. The family is essentially a conservative social unit that is sensitive to what is different, what is "foreign." The young therapist will have difficulty being paid attention to by older parents generally, but especially by older parents from a poor minority. In the same way, the female therapist will be paid less attention to than her male counterpart. The black therapist will have more difficult going with white families, and vice versa.

In both conversations with the residents I raise questions about the validity of the concept of family *systems*, and the concept of family *change*.

In regard to family *systems*, I think the term has become inoperable because it has been adopted by too many who represent really very divergent orientations in the field. Family *change* is most often inferred from changes in symptoms or conduct reported by or observed in family members. What the therapist observes or hears reports about is improved functioning in family members. It seems somewhat pointless to talk about family change when what we really hear about is individual change. But we work with the family process to bring about individual change.

Part III is "Interviews with Follow-up." The three chapters consist of my interviews with a family and a couple. In the beginning I describe certain characteristics of the family and the couple upon entering therapy, and at the end I comment on the interviews—suggest my strategies, as it were—and provide information about the outcome of the work done.

Chapter 1 of Part III consists of excerpts from interviews with a lower middle-class Jewish family composed of parents in their later middle age and two teenaged daughters. Both daughters refused to attend school, and so were referred by the school system to the Court of Philadelphia. Interviews with the family extended through about one year, after which there was a termination mainly initiated by the family. But four months after termination I again saw the family when I learned second-hand that one of my goals had been reached.

Chapters 2 and 3 of Part III are composed of interviews with my commentary with a young, lower middle-class, white Protestant couple. (The reader may be somewhat put off by my labeling families "Jewish," or "white Protestant," but these are facts about families that provide essential information about their styles and likely modes of response to therapy and/or therapist, and are not to be disregarded as anachronisms. Neither obviously are they intended to connote the whole story about a family or its members.) The wife had recently returned from a third runaway episode—an episode that had lasted two years. There was a total of ten interviews with the couple followed by a termination despite my request for continuation on an infrequent basis. The couple exhibited increasing good feeling and cooperativeness in the course of the interviews. Unfortunately the atmosphere of good will broke down several months after termination, and the wife again left her husband. But in this leaving she did something different: this time, she took her children with her. In prior episodes she had left the children to her husband and mother-in-law. About a year after termination the husband telephoned to ask me to see him and his wife again. But after telephone conversations with his wife, who seemed to me conducting herself in a relatively mature manner under difficult circumstances, I declined to see the couple. This is not a successful textbook case, but it is a reminder that the relationship of therapist and family does not cease upon termination. It may be restored at certain critical junctures in family life, and the therapist must decide whether and to what extent to allow its restoration.

The three sections of this book represent my views on family therapy expressed in different contexts: in the first, the written clinical essay; in the second, the rather informal interchange characteristic of the training seminar; and in the third, the therapy interview. I believe the different frameworks reflect a single viewpoint. What a therapist does in interviews should be discerned in his written formulations about what he does in interviews. Inconsistency there may be—and I suspect it will be pointed out to me— but my impression is that consistency predominates.

The work reported here evolves from my membership over a twelve year period in the Family Psychiatry Department at Eastern Pennsylvania Psychiatric Institute in Philadelphia—currently as Associate Director for Training in the Department.

Part I, with minor changes, and the first two chapters of Part III, with minor changes, were recorded for an audiocassette series entitled *Family Therapy and Diagnosis*, published in 1973 by Psychiatry and Behavioral Science Associates, Haverford, Pennsylvania. The transcripts in Parts II and III required editing to improve syntax, to make them more readable. A version of Chapter 1 of Part I is in *Group Therapy*, edited by Lewis Wolberg and Marvin Aronson (1974, pp. 34–44).

GERALD H. ZUK

PART I

CONCEPTS AND CLASSIFICATIONS

CHAPTER 1

ENGAGEMENT AND TERMINATION AS CRITICAL INCIDENTS IN THERAPY

All schemata do some injustice to the information they are supposed to organize; the best probably do the least. A useful schema in psychotherapy is to organize it into beginning, middle and ending phases and describe characteristics of each phase. The problem in applying the beginning, middle and ending schema to family therapy is that transitions often occur too rapidly to divide meaningfully; that some family therapy contacts are very brief; and that its goals must be multiple. Personality restructuring (including the notion of self-other differentiation), the major stated goal of psychoanalysis, is unrealistic in most family therapy work; and symptom-reduction, the major stated goal of most behavior therapy, while desirable is not the only desirable goal or the most desirable.

Among the desirable goals of family therapy must be considered conflict-resolution, improved understanding and communication among members, an enhanced family solidarity, but also a greater tolerance for and appreciation of individuality.

Phases of Family Therapy

In my view family therapy consists of a series of critical incidents beginning with the engagement. The engagement is a critical incident in family therapy in part because of the presence of persons who do not consider themselves patients. The level of anxiety in these persons as well as in the person designated as the patient is likely to be high, and so it is necessary for the therapist to take steps to control the anxiety lest it drive them away.

I consider the engagement the prototype of critical incidents in family therapy, which is the reason I will focus on it in this paper. In a sense all others are reenactments of the engagement. Other critical incidents include an engagement phase followed by points of rising tension as therapist and family negotiate the "issue"—i.e., the substance or content of the incident. During the engagement and in succeeding critical incidents, there are moments at which the risk of termination is increased, and termination of therapy may actually occur. Termination is another critical incident in family therapy, and will also be a topic of discussion here. Some psychotherapies consider it a kind of weaning period; but in family therapy termination must, like engagement, be considered a phase of active negotiation between therapist and family in which the most significant therapeutic change may be recorded.

The Engagement

My remarks on engagement are limited to cases in which families are seen in an outpatient-type setting; in which a referral has been made usually by a staff member of a community agency, such as a school counselor; in which an initial appointment has been scheduled over the telephone with a family member, usually a wife or mother; and in which the member has been instructed to bring to the initial interview all family members residing in the home. My procedure on engagement does *not* vary according to the length of contact I think the family may be inclined to accept. It is followed with all families and is designed to encourage engagement and continuation beyond. It is designed also to test motivation for therapy and to provide a base of information for the therapist's judgment regarding the possible course and outcome of therapy.

The prospect of the first interview produces anxiety in family members. This is natural for new situations, especially situations in which sensitive material is exchanged. Not all of the family members will accept the notion they are patients in the way the symptomatic member is. The requirement that the family participate in the interview is a powerful message communicated by the therapist regarding his notion of causation. The members' acceptance is really an acquiescence to his message that there is a kind of collective guilt operating, a wrongdoing that needs correction. Already the burden begins to shift from the offending (i.e., the symptomatic) member.

I avoid reviewing material that may be available about the family or the symptomatic member, because to do so can often set up a bias which interferes with proper evaluation based on the family interview. I may review such material after the first interview, when the effect of the bias will be reduced.

I ask what the problem is and who referred the family. I am interested in who takes the initiative to answer these inquiries. In American families they tend to be answered by the wife (if it is a couple in the interview) or the mother (if it is a couple plus children), because the wife-mother seems to be the spokesman, perhaps reflecting a centrality of the wife-mother in the nuclear family that seems to me expanding at the same time as the husband-father becomes more peripheral. It is accepted that wives have been the emotional core of the family, particularly as regards the relationship with children, but the extent of her centrality currently in the nuclear family may not be clearly recognized.

My motive in the initial meeting is to create interest in the family for a second meeting; and in the second meeting, interest for a third, and so on. Thus I am not so interested in the first few meetings in eliciting a detailed history as I am in mobilizing positive motivation to seal the engagement and continuation beyond. I tell the family that one meeting is not sufficient to establish the basis for therapy; several will be needed, after which it should be possible to state the way I view the problem and whether therapy will be recommended. I stress my interest in having the family pass through a brief series of evaluation meetings, usually giving the number as three or four.

I encourage family members to give their views on the problem, and to comment on each other's views, for sometimes interesting divergencies can appear on the nature of the problem. I am interested in which member characteristically corrects, revises, amends or otherwise monitors other members. I am especially interested in which silencing strategies exist in the family, or what other examples of pathogenic relating exist.

Families will sometimes disregard the instruction to bring all members residing at home. One mother who had a drug-taking young adult son left at home another 13-year-old son, stating that she did not want to involve the younger in the older son's troubles. I insisted she bring the younger son at least through the evaluation series. She asked if she should tell the younger son about his brother. I replied that he already probably knew more than she thought. I also told the mother I was not in favor of revealing all secrets in families; that it is appropriate to keep some information from children because to reveal it would evoke too much anxiety.

My practice is to conduct an evaluation series lasting three or four interviews, at which point a decision is made regarding continuation. Frequently it is clear by that time that the family is cooperative and that they are capable of responding well in the therapy situation. The decision to continue need not be formally conveyed; the next session is simply scheduled and the therapist may give some indication of the number of sessions and the period of time needed for useful change to occur. In the majority of cases, it is useful for the therapist to indicate how long he believes the therapy will take, and what changes he hopes will occur. He will want to convey some notion of conditions that may affect the length and outcome of therapy. This spelling out seems to me especially important in the case of lower class and many poor minority families, because in their minds therapy is closely associated with experience with physicians who prescribe medication.

Interpretation can have the effect of raising or lowering anxiety; but in the case of lower class families more often it raises anxiety, so I avoid making interpretations. Of course almost any comment by the therapist can be regarded as an interpretation, but he should exercise special caution in labeling motives not readily acknowledged by family members, especially when the motives imply bad will, manipulativeness, aggressiveness or animosity in members toward one another. Lower class families also do not tolerate well the therapist's demand for recall of past events, or to reminisce about the past. In initial interviews especially, the therapist is advised to soft-pedal such demands.

In the first few sessions the therapist tries to establish a friendly relation with the family while establishing also the legitimacy of his role as an expert and authority. He cannot take the friendly relation or his acceptance as an expert for granted, but must work toward each. For example, Jewish families characteristically subject the therapist to tests regarding his expertise, although once his role is accepted they make a good, perhaps the best response in therapy. Black families, on the other hand, are likely to invest the therapist with too much power, and react negatively when he calls attention to his limitations; or they leave treatment prematurely once tensions or symptoms have been reduced. The therapist who shares the religious, ethnic or racial background of the family has an advantage over the one who does not, although that does not solve all his problems.

In the first few sessions the therapist and family try to come to some agreement over the hour and day of sessions, the fee and frequency of sessions, deciding which members must be present and which can be excused. In lower class families in particular, fathers may complain that they cannot take time from their employment. This is another issue to be discussed and resolved. The resolution of these items, which can appear to be so incidental to the therapy, may have the most significant effect on outcome, for they require negotiation between the therapist and family and, from my point of view, therapeutic change is an outcome of negotiation. The family is not a blank slate to be written on at will by the therapist. Every family therapy is really a contest between therapist and family as to who will change the other, and how; and under what circumstances. Families *assert* themselves against the therapist; they are not simply passive units waiting to be acted upon. Change arises out of the various *contests* between therapist and family. Sometimes families change only after they have perceived a change in the therapist. Sometimes families change only after they have demonstrated to their satisfaction the therapist's lack of skill, as is sometimes the case when they leave therapy against the therapist's advice.

Even the gifted therapist will lose his share of families during the engagement, particularly lower class and poor minority families which are prone to impose narrow criteria on what may happen in therapy and what its outcomes may be. All families enter therapy with a high level of anxiety which must be controlled lest it drive them away prematurely. Sealing the engagement is the first goal of family therapy, and the therapist's main effort must be directed toward controlling the family's anxiety level during the engagement phase.

The Termination

There are many kinds of termination in family therapy, as in other psychotherapies. Each interview may be described as having an engagement phase and a termination phase, although this is not what therapists ordinarily mean by these terms. They usually refer to the goals or outcomes of a series of interviews:—in the case of the engagement, the first series; in the case of the termination, the last.

The main point I wish to make about termination in family therapy is that it is, like the engagement, a phase of active negotiation between therapist and family, containing marked potential for therapeutic change. It should not be perceived mainly as a weaning period, as in some psychotherapies, but really as another contest in a series of contests between therapist and family regarding needed change. Sometimes the therapist will introduce the issue of termination as a challenge to the family, as a means to induce change. Sometimes the family will introduce the issue of termination, as a means to maintain the status quo or as a device to cause the therapist to reduce his demands.

The therapist works to take the decision to terminate out of the hands of the family. My practice to have an evaluation series consisting of three or four interviews is part of my effort to discourage premature termination. It is a brief series which allows the family and me to get acquainted. The decision at the end of the series may be that therapy is not needed at the time; or that a referral elsewhere is indicated; or that therapy for a certain length of time and number of interviews is indicated but that it will be limited to the parental couple and not include children. The evaluation series is short enough to contain the anxiety regarding a long-term commitment, but long enough to generate an attitude of interest in and liking for the therapist and therapy situation.

Any change noticed by family members, or the absence of change, may be used as grounds for termination by the members. A disagreement between therapist and family regarding what needs changing can also be the basis for the family's seeking termination. The therapist may not be directly confronted, but the family misses interviews that have been scheduled, or certain members may not show up for interviews. My policy, as I stated before, is to take the decision to terminate out of the hands of the family; so I will call a family that misses appointments uncooperative and say that I am not obligated to continue work with the family. This sudden reversal, which takes the initiative for termination out of the hands of the family, can have the effect of restoring a more constructive attitude toward continuation. Families will sometimes test the therapist's need for *them* by threatening termination. This poses a special problem for the therapist by testing his self-assurance and sense of worth.

The therapist may decide to terminate with a family when one of his goals has been achieved, although not all his goals, on the assumption that the family is not ready for the type of interaction or direction that is needed to achieve the other goals. He may state this as the case to the family, while offering to be available for further work at a later time when there is greater readiness. Some families react with confusion or regret at this position and may try to convince the therapist, directly or by indirect means, that he should continue the therapy. Once in a while the convincing may take the form of a sudden dramatic improvement in a member's functioning. The therapist needs to evaluate such sudden, unexpected changes in the light of his over-all goals, and decide if the surprise changes provide sufficient evidence that those goals may be obtained.

Obviously the therapist does not introduce the subject of termination lightly, or simply as a trick to dissipate resistance to change. He does so only when he has exhausted other sources of leverage available to him, or when he is convinced that an impasse exists in the therapy that seriously impairs his effectiveness.

In a recent case I broached termination to a couple when, after several months of weekly interviews, it appeared that the husband, who had been hospitalized briefly a third time for a psychotic episode, was unable to accept my demand that he return to full-time employment. The couple made progress in the therapy: they were able to discuss disagreements and were more cooperative with each other; and the husband was relatively symptom-free. But he was fearful of returning to full-time work lest he have another psychotic episode or fail at the job. As it was, he was receiving a level of financial support from welfare agencies that nearly equalled his salary as a full-time worker. Not wishing to use the therapy to support the status quo, I declined further work with the couple while recommending other helping sources. I think termination is legitimate when circumstances outside the therapy impose severe limitations which restrict its goals.

Once in a while I receive evidence from families of a significant change occurring *after* termination, which I concluded was a result of the termination and of having been in therapy. Sometimes although there is a rising potential for change in the course of the therapy, it fails to materialize; or a goal especially desired by the therapist fails to be achieved. It seems to me that termination may free families or family members for change for which they were ready, but which for various reasons could not occur while in the therapy situation.

In a Jewish, middle class oriented family composed of parents and their two teenaged daughters, both of whom were high school dropouts, one of my goals was accomplished after the family terminated. During about a year of therapy in which we had twenty-five interviews, there were positive results: the emotional atmosphere was less depressive. However one of my main goals, the return of both girls to some type of regular schooling, was not achieved before termination. The initiative in this case for termination came mainly from the family: one of the daughters decided to take a summer job outside the city and would not be able to attend further interviews. Although I encouraged continuation upon her return from the job, I doubted that there would be.

Four months after termination I received a telephone call from a local vocational training school informing me that both daughters had applied there, and that the younger had already started the program. On the basis of this information I requested a follow-up evaluation with the family, which the members agreed to. During the follow-up, interestingly enough, everyone agreed that gains had been made during the course of therapy, but they were lost at termination. The daughters denied a relation between the therapy and their interest in vocational training.

Excluding a family member from attending further interviews is a kind of selective termination which can have a powerful therapeutic effect. In one case I asked parents, after several months of once-weekly interviews, to leave their son at home or in school. They were surprised because the son was the symptomatic member. But by this device I hoped to reinforce a message I had communicated several times verbally already: that the central problem lay in the relationship of the parents; the son's disturbed behavior was merely an offshoot. The exclusion was a strong reinforcement at the *action* level of the verbal message.

Types of Family Therapy

Table 1 describes characteristics of some types of family therapy. Family therapy can be very brief, as in the crisis-resolution type; or it can be long-term (although not long-term according to the requirements for psycho-analysis). Chart 1 is a hypothetical chart, to be sure, but it is based on extensive clinical experience with a wide variety of families presenting a variety of behavioral and/or psychiatric problems. The chart helps make clear my

TABLE 1

Characteristics of Some Types of Family Therapy

Types	No. Contacts	Family Characteristics	Goals
Crisis-resolution	1-6 interviews over 1 to 6 weeks	Disorganized; many poor minority	Primarily to reduce tensions
Short-term	10-15 interviews over 2½ to 4 months	Lower middle-class	Primarily symptom-reduction
Middle-range	25-30 interviews over 6 to 8 months	Middle-class	Better communication and understanding among family members
Long-term	40 or more interviews over 10 to 15 months	Middle- and upper middle-class	Increased solidarity but with better acceptance of individuality in members

view that only, perhaps, in the case of long-term family therapy would it be appropriate to employ a schema such as the beginning, middle and ending phases of psychotherapy.

Crisis-resolution

Many family therapy cases are precipitated by a crisis. Either a member becomes seriously symptomatic, in the psychiatric sense; or the behavior of a member becomes unmanageable; or a member violates a community code—for example, becomes assaultive and is apprehended by the police. Typically in this type of case there are one to six interviews over one to six weeks. The family often presents a picture of disorganization; often it is a one-parent family, and often a poor minority family. The therapist's goal is to reduce tension and if possible resolve the crisis. Despite the best efforts of therapists, most of these families will not continue once tension-reduction or crisis-resolution has occurred.

Short-term

The length of many family therapy cases is limited by the families' rather pragmatic definition of the problem to be dealt with, and by the reluctance of these families to be involved over a long period of time in any enterprise requiring extensive verbal exchange. Black families tend to decline long-term involvement, and exhibit numerous strategies designed to limit the length of the therapy contact. But many white "blue-collar" families are also not comfortable "just sitting and talking," and so take steps to limit the length of therapy. Short-term therapy families generally demand that the goal of therapy be limited to symptom-reduction. Typically they are seen in from ten to fifteen interviews extending over two-and-a-half to four months.

Middle-range

Middle-class families frequently do not have a fixed notion of what therapy ought to accomplish, nor is the notion usually so pragmatically cure-oriented as in the case of lower-class and many minority families. They are willing to look upon therapy as a learning experience as well as a strictly therapeutic one in the medical sense of the term. Thus they will not set such strict limits on the time for therapy and will be sympathetic to broader goals than, generally speaking, will lower-class and many poor minority families. Middle-range families, according to my chart, are typically seen from twenty-five to thirty interviews extending over six to eight months.

Long-term

Jewish families, coming from a culture that values words and skillful exchange of words highly, and admiring those that use words well, are often quite favorable cases for long-term family therapy. Other relatively more sophisticated middle- and upper middle-class families may also be quite favorably disposed. The goal of long-term therapy usually requires a family that exhibits a fair degree of existing solidarity, in which the problem may be the solidarity itself. I perceive the goal of long-term therapy as enhancing solidarity but with increased tolerance and understanding of individuality.

All family therapy deals with and attempts to alter values in members, but long-term therapy especially. In a recent case, the depression of a young man and his poor marital adjustment seemed to me related to his acceptance of the *value*, probably derived basically from a parent but by way of other authority figures also, that a man had to make his mark in the world by the age of 30 or he was a failure. The acceptance of this value, this notion about how life had to be lived, its worthwhile goals, was literally driving the young man and his wife crazy because the fact was that he had not made his mark. Therapy must be an inquiry into the values held by family members, and an effort to change values that are unsuitable or inappropriate in the sense that they are contributory causes to psychiatric symptoms or disturbed behavior.

This type of therapy may last forty or more interviews over a period of from ten to fifteen months.

My experience in the outpatient setting has not led to optimism regarding the value of family therapy lasting beyond fifteen months. Some therapists have voiced optimistic opinions, but my experience suggests that even well-motivated families decline to continue beyond that period; and even if the therapist is insistent, families will take steps to precipitate a termination. My position is also colored by views regarding goals in family therapy: personality change is not realistic, although I think it sometimes occurs in the course or aftermath of therapy. Symptom-reduction is a realistic goal, although one aims for more than that, hopeful of reducing pernicious group process that has contributed to tensions leading to symptoms.

Cases can be selected for special study beyond the 15-month level. The therapist may want to learn about a particular type of family, or about the process of therapy. A favorable case for this type of special study is the hospitalized schizophrenic or psychotic and his family, because hospitalization creates leverage to increase family cooperation for an extended family therapy. Most of those who have treated hospitalized schizophrenics or psychotics and their families over a long period of time, while recognizing the value of the work as a learning experience, would probably be reluctant to voice enthusiasm with regard to outcome.

CHAPTER 2

ON PATHOGENIC RELATING, THE CELEBRANT,
AND VALUES IN THERAPY

Two concepts described previously and basic to my notion of a triadic-based family therapy, seem to me in need of further elaboration. These are pathogenic relating—a diagnosis of family malfunctioning; and go-between process—a concept and technique of therapy.

Pathogenic relating refers to the therapist's judgment regarding unproductive, tension-producing, intimidating, malevolent patterns in families which can trigger psychiatric symptoms and other behavior disturbances. The discussion will follow two directions: the first will be a discussion in greater depth than before of the basis for judging pathogenic relating. It cannot be derived from verbal report about family conflict, or from the history directly, or from presenting symptoms; but it is rather a product, an outcome of the relationship that develops between the therapist and family.

The other discussion on pathogenic relating will be a consideration of the antagonism that exists between the nuclear family and other social systems—more specifically, the implications of that antagonism for the therapist working with families. The centrality of the wife-mother in interviews with families is impressive, as is the emotional loyalty to her of her children. She is the core of the nuclear family, while she holds a peripheral position in other social systems dominated by men. In the nuclear family the husband-father is peripheral, and the trend in the past decade or two may be that he has become more so.

The discussion on go-between process will also take two directions. The first will describe a third role for the family therapist in addition to two I described previously (the go-between and side-taker). The third role or function I will call that of celebrant. As celebrant the therapist is a special kind of mediator between the family and the community. Rather like a judge, priest or civic official, he is often called on to officiate at or "celebrate" an event that has been deemed important by the family, such as a death or birth, a separation or reconciliation, a runaway or return from runaway of a family member, a hospitalization or release from hospitalization, a loss or recovery of a job. As celebrant the therapist confirms and signifies that the event did indeed occur. The therapist may attempt to expand his functions to the others I have talked about (the go-between and side-taker) but the

13

family may have so narrowly prescribed his function that it will terminate the contact if he attempts it.

The second discussion with respect to go-between process is grounded in my observation that, despite the wide variety of conflicts expressed in interviews, there are really three main categories: (1) the conflict regarding appropriate sex roles, especially as enacted between husband and wife; (2) the conflict regarding appropriate age roles, especially as enacted between parents and children; and (3) the conflict regarding the appropriate relationship of the family to the community, as enacted especially in frictions relating to a cluster of social class factors including race, religion, education and job status. The therapist will be called upon to take positions with regard to these main categories; he will not be able to avoid taking sides, so he must be prepared to respond according to a *rational* scheme. When he sides with the husband in conflict with his wife, with parents in conflict with their children, and with the community in conflict with the family, the therapist expresses what I refer to as "discontinuity values." When he sides with the wife, the children and the family in the conflicts, according to my view the therapist is espousing "continuity values."

The therapist will note a concordance among the values expressed by husbands, parents and community compared with those expressed by wives, children and family in relation to the major categories of conflict expressed in family interviews: the husband-wife conflict, the parent-child conflict, and the family-community conflict. There is a commonality in the sets of values expressed by husband and wife, by parents and children, and by family and community as they struggle to be needed, to be loved, to control and acquire power and authority in their relationships with each other. One set, referred to as "discontinuity values," emphasizes rational order, system, definitions, rules and procedures, selectivity and exclusivity. The other set, "continuity values," deemphasizes order, system, definitions, etc.; it espouses an egalitarianism mixed with an anti-uniformity. In expressing their conflicts with one another, it is surprising how predictably husbands, parents and community agents will espouse the "discontinuity values;" and how wives, children and families will espouse the "continuity values." The predictability is useful knowledge for the family therapist who must make important decisions regarding which set of values to side with.

I. Pathogenic Relating

A. Basis for Judging Pathogenic Relating

While the report of family members on conflict affects the evaluation, in itself the report is not pathogenic relating. Nor is the recounting of the family history, although it too may be a contributor to the therapist's evaluation. The presence of symptoms or expression of intense affect are not in themselves pathogenic relating, although they may be elements.

Pathogenic relating is a judgment made by the therapist regarding tension-producing, malevolent, intimidating patterns of family members toward each other *and the therapist* as he observes it in interviews. When he misses or cannot observe it directly, the therapist can stimulate pathogenic relating by various means including suggestion, teasing, prodding, exhorting, side-taking, silencing, task-assigning, and threatening to suspend sessions or terminate therapy.

Silencing strategies constitute pathogenic relating of the kind that can ordinarily be observed frequently and early in therapy. But the report by a family member about how he is silenced by others is not sufficient for the therapist. He wants to see and hear the process erupt before him; that is, to be in its presence when it occurs and if necessary be the spur for its occurrence. He wants to observe the response of the so-called victim. Does the victim fall silent or explode with rage? Does he plead with his silencers or castigate them? Does he show somatic symptoms such as flushing or trembling? Or does he show such inappropriate behavior as silly smiling, giggling, or laughter?

Not infrequently the therapist finds himself joined in the pathogenic relating as a constituent element. Family members exert pressure which he experiences as tension in himself. For example, he suddenly finds himself angry at a member and wishing to retaliate. (I am not talking about counter-transference, but about an understandable response to what is a calculated assault upon the therapist.) The therapist may find himself restrained from introducing certain topics, or from confronting a member on a certain issue. He may find himself being forced to take sides with a scapegoated member, and experiencing the same silencing that that member has at the hands of other family members. When the therapist experiences these pressures and reacts to them; when he observes that they follow more or less regularly some sort of planned cooperative effort on the part of family members; when the outcome of the interaction is frequently one in which somebody in the family begins to act a little crazy, then I think it is proper for him to conclude that he has been in the presence of pathogenic relating, and that he has experienced a pattern which family members have become used to and quite skillful at with each other and outsiders.

Pathogenic relating directed at the therapist by families usually takes the form of pressuring him to take sides prematurely, either with one faction of the family against another or with the family as a whole against some outside agency or institution. (At the end of each interview, the *second* question the therapist should ask himself is, "What did they tell me that was new today?" The *first* is, "With whom or on what issue did they expect me to take sides?" In other words, information about the *relationship* of the therapist to family members takes precedence over other kinds of information). Members wish to persuade the therapist that another member is really crazy and needs to be in a hospital. Or members seek to persuade the therapist that there is no problem in the family at all; rather the problem rests in an unreasonable, irrational or intimidating attitude on the part of a referring agency such as the school system, courts or police department. The family's attitude is that it is being victimized by the outside agency, and it wishes the therapist to side with its position against the agency.

Family pressure on the therapist to accept its view of the problem prematurely may constitute pathogenic relating, which may also be the case when it places the full burden on him to define the problem. In the first instance the therapist is pressured to take the family's side in viewing the problem. In the second instance, the family wishes to make it appear that (1) there is no problem, or (2) the problem is a whim of the therapist and the family is obedient to his whim.

With families who insist that the therapist accept their definition of the problem; or who deny the existence of a problem; or who demand the therapist formulate it without adequate information and cooperation, my practice is to describe therapy as serious business and to question the seriousness of the family. I state that I cannot undertake the work without a conviction that the family shares my notion of its seriousness, and that I must become convinced by the time the evaluation series is completed, which is usually by the end of three or four interviews. This is a tactic which I find necessary with some families and useful in restoring a balance favorable to the therapist's work. It can turn aside a form of pathogenic relating which can seriously undermine chances of a good outcome. The family, puzzled by the therapist's demand to be serious and searching for his definition of seriousness, is sidetracked from its effort to subvert.

Characteristically in interviews I ask family members to tell me what happened to them during the preceding week (usually I schedule sessions, at least at the beginning of therapy, at weekly intervals). What problems arose? What arguments? Did anything unusual happen on the way to the interview? Did anything special happen on the way back from the last? (If the answers are negative, I persist with: "Tell me what happened anyway.") The recounting of what happened may consume the entire time or very little. If I do not think it provides a rich enough base for my possible interventions, I will change the subject. I may return to an event that occurred in the family weeks previously, and ask for current reactions. Sometimes pathogenic relating will consist of an attempt by the family to divert me from my procedure. If I ask what happened during the previous week, I am told what happened five years ago; or what is likely to happen in the future if things keep on as they are. Members may say something important happened, but they can't recall what it was. Or just as one member is to relate an important event of the past week, he is interrupted by another. Of course the therapist must try to shortcircuit these interferences, although he may encounter sharp resistance when he attempts to do so. I assume that these sidetracking tactics do not originate in the therapy, although there may be novel elements due to the therapy situation; but that they are more or less characteristic disruptive patterns which appear when family members are under stress and when danger to the status quo is experienced.

Ordinarily in families the therapist is exposed to many examples of pathogenic relating, not just one. They may arise as a result of his active intervention, or simply as a result of his presence. In his presence two family members may interact in such a way that one becomes a bit crazy. For example, a husband accuses his wife of being an inadequate, uncaring mother and wife. She turns away from him and weeps quietly. Seeing this he becomes disorganized and begins to babble; that is, he starts to talk about events in a manner that strikes the therapist as inappropriate. One can presume that, as a result of his accusation, the husband calculated that his wife would be hurt. But his wife exhibits her hurt in such a manner as to produce in her husband an inappropriate response, i.e., he becomes a bit crazy. I think one can presume that this sort of interaction has happened before, perhaps many times, and that its usual outcome was for the *husband* to become a bit crazy rather than the wife—that is, the outcome was not random.

In the case of a young Orthodox rabbi and his wife seen because the wife felt lonely, nervous and depressed, in the first few interviews I found myself engaged with the couple in two types of interactions that seemed to me to contain elements of pathogenic relating. In both instances I was pressured to take sides prematurely; in essence, to show a loyalty based on a very new fragile relationship. In the first instance, husband and wife bombarded each other with accusations. Then each would turn to me and ask: "Who is right?" In order to understand the second type of pathogenic relating, it is necessary to relate that the young rabbi, struggling with his first poorly attended synagogue and having to meet the needs of a growing family, but also being prone to undertake too many activities prematurely, found himself in the position of believing he had to accept welfare payments from the state. The welfare department, increasingly reluctant to provide him with the level of support he had been receiving, was demanding more evidence of need. I came to understand that part of his motivation for therapy was to provide evidence of need to the welfare department. Husband and wife pressured me to write to the welfare department on their behalf. This I refused to do, although I agreed to a note stating the couple was beginning therapy. My refusal obviously upset the couple and appointments began to be missed. The rabbi and his wife finally did attend another interview during which I confronted them with my belief they were using the therapy in an unjustified way. Despite strenuous objection, I held to this position and stated furthermore that in the absence of genuine cooperation and a serious attitude, I would have to suspend work. This interview in which the confrontation took place seemed to be a turning point. In subsequent interviews, the level of cooperation sharply increased, and the rabbi and his wife dropped the issue of welfare payments. In particular the wife reported that she and her husband actually spent a week without arguments—something she could not recall in her memory of their relationship.

I would maintain that the rabbi and his wife pressured me in a manner that was not new but simply a repetition of a pattern they had developed with each other and outsiders. The pattern generated anxiety; it was one in which recrimination played a large role; and it was intended to generate a sense of guilt in the so-called victim. My response was calculated to disrupt the pattern; that is, to undo one link in this chain of pathogenic relating.

In another case, pathogenic relating developed in the aftermath of a couple's attempt to enlist my aid in continuing their dependence on tranquillizing medication. At first the couple refused to consider therapy as anything but a base to secure medication but later, after a contest with them over the definition of therapy, it was possible to dislodge their notion. They made progress once they were able to turn their attention to other issues in their lives.

In still another case, pathogenic relating was involved in a husband's effort to get me to side with him in order to continue to receive benefits from welfare agencies that were providing him with an amount equal to about two-thirds of his regular income prior to his hospitalization for a psychotic episode. Upon release from the hospital, he was referred for therapy with his wife. He was functioning reasonably well at home and appeared cooperative in interviews until I suggested that it would be consistent with the role of husband and father to return to fulltime employment. He expressed the fear that, should he find work and then lose it as a result of having another episode, he might lose the welfare payments on which he had come to depend so heavily. I saw husband and wife for fourteen interviews, hopeful of persuading him to return to fulltime work, but declined further interviews when it became apparent he would not. I suggested other sources of help that might be available to him and his wife, but declined to continue therapy in the belief it was being used mainly to support the status quo.

B. Antagonisms that Underlie Pathogenic Relating

Although there may be many goals in family therapy, I believe there is only one central goal: the reduction and replacement of pathogenic relating. The central aim of the therapist must be, in my opinion, to return the family to functioning "within normal limits." For each family, a judgment of what constitutes "within normal limits" must be made by the therapist, in the same way that he must decide when readiness for change is not present or not sufficient so that a course of therapy should not be undertaken.

"Within normal limits" for me does not mean the absence of frictions, rivalries or competition between husband and wife, parents and children, between one family and another or one family and the community. It does not mean the absence of anxiety, guilt, frustration, anger or bitterness. It does not mean that fair play is always present in the associations of family members. It does not necessarily mean that family members feel a common bond of sympathy or understanding, or have developed a sense of solidarity but yet with appreciation of individual differences.

"Within normal limits" means for me that these malevolent, intimidating, disruptive, inflammatory processes referred to as pathogenic relating are no longer observed by the therapist, or that they have been reduced, and that with reduction or elimination has come a noticeable improvement in family relations and/or individual functioning. The therapist need not stop his work at this point. As a preventive measure he may wish to continue with the family. But my point is that his main professional obligation has been met. Case-by-case experience suggests little support for the notion that one moves to so-called larger, more pervasive goals such as personality transformation. Therapists who support such a notion have a great burden to document it for students and others.

Desirable but not central also are other sorts of goals, such as restoration of a marriage or improvement of job status or better school achievement. These may occur as pathogenic relating is reduced. But it is one of the most serious entrapments of the therapist to side prematurely with a husband to save a marriage, or with a wife to hold her husband in his job, or with a parent to improve a child's poor school performance. Generally speaking, therapists should steer clear of communicating goals to families in terms of preventing separations or divorce, or improving job or school performance.

Each family interview after the initial meeting begins with my question, "Well, and what happened to you this week?" As members respond, I try to get details about those events that produced friction or conflict. As members provide details, I try to assess the status of pathogenic relating. I am curious as to whether members are responding differently to provocations from other members. I am curious as to whether certain types of events that have had a high probability of occurring weekly in the family suddenly decrease. I am curious as to whether the members are responding to me in a novel manner; for example, with less demand for siding or less provocatively in other ways. And I am interested in whether members are making new demands of each other or me.

Although wide departures are often unavoidable, I believe the optimum interview length is 40 minutes. That is, in 40 minutes the therapist should be able to test the status of current relationships by asking members to review the events of the past few days or more; to select out certain themes suggested by the members' recall; to relate those themes to his evolving concept of pathogenic relating in the family; and to take a position (or not), or reconfirm a position, on what seems promising as leverage against the pathogenic relating.

I try to make a judgment regarding when the family's exchanges during interviews begin to fall more "within normal limits." As in a recent case, this may strike me as the point at which a wife says about her husband: "Doctor, he is back where he was before he got sick. He's mean; he says terrible things to me. If this is what he is when he's better, how can I live with him?" Her husband, hospitalized for a depressive episode, was improved and returned to fulltime work. The wife, rather depressed when her husband was in the hospital, was also improved. Both reduced the amount of medication they were receiving to control depression and anxiety. But serious complaints about the marriage continued. The wife charged her husband cared little for her or the children. The husband resented her accusations and said she was ungrateful and too demanding. The therapy continued, not because of the unhappiness expressed in the marriage, but rather because the pattern identified as pathogenic relating, although reduced, was still evident to me in family interviews.

In daily life there are numerous antagonisms that provide sources of power that generate pathogenic relating. In family interviews three main categories of antagonisms are apparent: (1) the male-female struggle, especially evident in conflicts between husband and wife; (2) the parent-child struggle, especially evident in conflicts between male children and their parents; and (3) the social status struggle, especially evident in conflicts of the husband at work and in family-neighborhood disputes. Although there are literally hundreds of conflicts aired in family interviews, these are three main categories under which they may be distributed.

The frictions between husband and wife in everyday living can generate sparks of pathogenic relating when one or the other—usually, of course, the wife—consolidates the loyalty of her children and presents a solid front opposite her husband. The frictions between parents and children can generate sparks when one, particularly a male child, attracts his mother into siding with him in a quasi-sexual relation bound to engender resentment and jealousy on the part of the father. The frictions encountered by a husband on his job can generate sparks when his wife, mobilizing the support of the children, declines to give sympathy in his search for new employment and threatens to leave him if he persists in his hunt. Doubtless also that fortuitous events, such as the birth of a physically or mentally handicapped child, or a financial crisis, or the revelation of a shocking secret, can provide the necessary spark to generate pathogenic relating.

Much of the pathogenic relating I observe in family interviews is, in my opinion, causally related to a current condition of the nuclear family unit in which the husband-father has been nearly extruded. In many instances today the nuclear family as a functioning entity is made up of the wife-mother and children with the husband as a peripheral or absent figure. Technological and economic pressures during the first half of this century undoubtedly served to unhinge the nuclear family from its close tie with the extended family system. The husband-father's role was already weakened in this period, if for no other reason than that the extended family system endorsed a nuclear family unit in which the husband-father played an integral role. During the past two decades, as a result of continuing pressures from the technology and economy, but with new pressures from the information explosion brought on by jet travel, television, computers and the like, the husband-father's role in the nuclear unit has further deteriorated. He is further alienated from wife and children with the result that children are more completely under control of the wife. Her attitudes, emotional tone, values and style sway her children more than they did even two or three decades ago. The attitudes, values, emotional tone and style of the husband-father are more distrusted by children than they were two or three decades ago.

Figure 1 is a graphic presentation of hypothesized changes in the nuclear family over the past few decades in the United States. Part B of Figure 1 in comparison with Part A indicates that the "buffer role" exercised by the combination of the father and extended family operating between the mother-child unit and societal agencies and institutions, has been reduced. To the extent the father and extended family remained significant viable units and reinforced each other, as I suggested they did in the more traditional family form, there was a check on the extent of diffusion of the mother's values to her children. But that check has diminished in the past few decades as a result of the reduced status of the extended family and of the father, and the mother has become an increasingly dominant teaching agent for her children. Traditionally her values have been at odds with those of societal agencies and institutions which are dominanted by male values. Her children, male and female, increasingly subject to her values as a result of the increasing separation of the father from the nuclear unit, are increasingly at odds with those most powerful endorsers of the father, societal agencies and institutions.

FIGURE 1

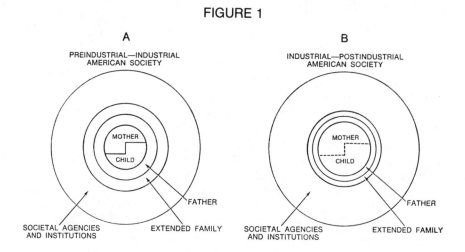

CHANGING RELATION OF
MOTHER-CHILD TO OTHER FAMILY AND SOCIAL SYSTEMS

In many instances today, the family therapist confronts a distraught, anguished mother who does not understand that the disturbed behavior of her children, especially her male children, is causally related to their over-responsiveness to her values, attitudes and style vis-à-vis those of their father—an over-responsiveness that has brought them into a collision-course with male-dominated societal agencies and institutions. It comes as something of a shock to learn that there is an antagonism between her values in the home with her children, and those of the male-dominated society; that to the extent her children become over-responsive to her values, they are at odds with those of the society, and their behavior will reflect the collision of values especially as they move into adolescence. While members of the women's liberation movement might not take kindly to my explanation of why father-alienation and father-absence are causes of behavior disturbances in children, I think they would agree that the society is dominated by male values; that women face a serious handicap competing with men; and that there is a deep sense of frustration and antagonism in women resulting from their unequal position.

It will be good for children to have their mothers less frustrated and antagonistic toward the society when measures are taken to equalize their opportunity. But it will be equally good for children when the society takes further steps to discourage father-alienation, father-separation or father-absence.

II. Go-Between Process

A. The Celebrant Role

I described go-between process as the therapist's application of leverage to displace pathogenic relating. The two sources of leverage were when the therapist acted as the go-between, and when he acted as side-taker. Both roles allow the therapist to initiate changes in family interaction. But I think also that there is a third source of leverage available to the therapist—when he acts in the role of celebrant.

It may be helpful to think of the celebrant as a transference-like phenomenon (in the psychoanalytic sense) in which the therapist is invested by family members with the mantles of those six well-known institutional father figures: (1) the priest (or minister or rabbi); (2) the judge; (3) the physician; (4) the policeman; (5) the lawyer; and (6) the politician.[1] But one must stop there with the transference notion. In family therapy it would be naive to think that transference exists "to be worked through," for the context is incompatible with the concept as originally intended. I even perceive a decline in the number of references to transference in some of the psychoanalytically-oriented family therapists in the past few years, which I interpret as disenchantment based on a failure of evidence.

Two types of cases provide the therapist with his best evidence of being cast as a celebrant: (1) lower class families; and (2) families interviewed at the point of crisis. Ordinarily regardless of the nature of the presenting problem, these are families which typically allow the therapist access for a

[1] These are celebrant roles which have been assigned me within my experience as a male therapist. I think a female therapist in addition would have to be prepared from time to time to assume the mantles of those well-known institutional *mother* figures: (1) the schoolteacher; and (2) the welfare worker or social service agent.

limited period of time. These are usually not long-term cases because, in the case of lower class families, while there is awe there is also a deep distrust of the therapist's expertise and an unwillingness to enter into a long-term relationship with an outsider who has superior education and sophistication. In the case of families seen at the point of crisis, there is a typical fixation on a symptomatic member who is creating the crisis. The short-term nature of such contacts is dictated by the difficulty encountered by the therapist— and frequently one that cannot be overcome—of shifting the focus away from the symptomatic member to others in the family.

"Short-term" families (i.e. lower class and "crisis-type" cases) are prone to demand from the therapist a specific type of service in a short time. But paradoxically within the restrictions imposed on type of service and time, "short-termers" are prone to overinflate the therapist's power and authority. The over-inflation often takes the form, because in American society the therapist is still an indefinite authority-expert, to attribute to him qualities of those much more familiar authorities—the priest, judge, physician, policeman, lawyer or politician. It helps provide closure for the "short-termers" to invest the therapist with the mantle of respect ordinarily accorded the priest, judge, etc.

As celebrant the therapist should recognize that he may be in a very powerful therapeutic position, but that he is in the position for a brief time only, and that he does not so much introduce change in family members as "celebrate" the fact that a change has occurred or is about to occur. The members, in a sense, empower him to certify that something has happened or is about to happen that is important to them, and thus it requires the presence and observance of a quasi-representative of one of the powerful institutions that make up society.

For example, the therapist may be used by a couple as a celebrant of the fact that they have elected to resume their married state after a separation. In one such instance in my experience, a wife returned to her husband after having left him a third time. I held ten interviews with the couple and then decided to suspend additional sessions because I concluded they would disrupt rather than further the healing process. I believed I had served to celebrate the couple's resumption of their marriage, and during the course of the ten sessions they gave me indications that they were taking the process seriously. The wife especially confirmed that she was acting responsibly toward her husband and children, and finding pleasure in being a wife and mother. She said she believed her husband's attitude was helpful in that he seemed to want her home and avoided condemning her for past actions. It was apparent the couple faced many problems in their new life together, and it was probable in the future they would be able to benefit from a therapy that addressed itself to an examination of conflicts and shortcomings, but for the present it seemed to me inadvisable to "accent the negative."

Of course one tests the readiness of family members to explore conflicts in depth, and there are times when the therapist can move from the celebrant role over to that of the go-between or side-taker. There are other times when, with families fully able to explore conflicts in depth and with whom he has developed go-between process by moving back and forth between the go-between role and that of the side-taker, the therapist suddenly finds himself cast in the celebrant role. He may find himself, as I have on occasion, explaining that he is *not* a lawyer or judge. Now when I find myself stating this to a family I suspect that it has wished to use me as a celebrant, and that I have implicitly recognized this by stating that I do *not* wish to be used that way. But whether the therapist wishes it or not, families will cast him as a celebrant on occasion. Indeed with certain families and in certain types of situations, that role is the only one available to him and he must make the most of it if he is to have any impact whatsoever. When the family decides he has truly celebrated the event for which he was sought, then it terminates no matter what the therapist may wish.

Elsewhere I have remarked that black lower-class families often cast the therapist as a quasi-political figure, such as a precinct captain or party committeeman; and that Jewish families are likely to cast him as a lawyer or judge. Thus the ethnic or racial factor is of significance in the kind of celebrant the therapist is to be. (I remember that many years ago as a clinical psychologist working in a heavily Catholic district in Philadelphia, occasionally I would find myself addressed by patients and their families as "Yes, Father—I mean, Doctor.") In some instances, not just with Catholic families, the therapist is clearly a quasi-priest who serves to facilitate a confession. A husband confesses a sexual affair to his wife. A father reveals to his children that he has served a jail term. Parents express their guilt at having obtained an abortion for their unmarried teenage daughter, and in effect ask forgiveness from the therapist. A child acknowledges for the first time to suspecting or unsuspecting parents that he has been using drugs. In the presence of the therapist-celebrant, these confessions can often be therapeutic experiences.

Earlier it was stated that one of the reasons the therapist is cast as celebrant is the brevity of the majority of family therapy cases. Specific examples used were the crisis-type cases and lower class families. In these cases the therapist is made celebrant because it is consistent with their expectations about therapy.

But there is another reason for the casting which has to do with the fact that the family, to a greater extent than the individual or other social units comprised of unrelated individuals, is a conservator—of heritage, of tradition, of ritual, of orthodoxy, of dogma. In the presence of his family, the individual finds himself more conservative than with outsiders. The special sense of well-being that many experience within their families may be due to the fact that the family's conservatism promotes security. The anxiety and emotional fatigue others experience when with families is because conservatism may also be threatening.

I wish to make the point that the therapist is cast as celebrant also because the family is a *conservative* unit. Conservatism requires families to expect that the therapist—whatever else he may be—will function as a quasi-representative of one of various powerful institutions that comprise society. Thus he is expected to act like minister or priest, physician or judge, etc.

Their conservatism means that families generally do not tolerate very well—especially in early interviews—a therapist's abrupt departure from their expectations about him as a quasi-priest, quasi-judge, quasi-physician, etc. For example, they do not tolerate very well the therapist who is profane, who is overly chummy, whose attire departs too much from the norm, whose suggestions or assignments strike them as foolish or absurd because they too sharply diverge from values held.

Also in accord with conservatism is the finding that some families simply will not tolerate a therapist under 40 years of age, or a female therapist, or a black therapist. Age, sex and race of the therapist are factors that turn some families off completely, although in the majority of cases this is not the fact.

Now all this may evoke in the reader the notion that I think family therapists should be "squares": this is far from the case; but it does mean that therapists will take special pains not to violate the conservatism that denotes the family. Therapists ignore this powerful factor at their own risk.

The family therapist as celebrant is a change agent in the sense that he helps seal a step in the process of change. He comes on the scene to testify that a change has occurred or is about to happen. With some families it is the only function he will be allowed, for they strictly delimit the type of access he will have.

B. "Continuity" versus "Discontinuity" Values Expressed by the Therapist and Family

The beginning family therapist is the victim of an information explosion; he suffers from a wealth of data. The problem is to sort out and to make good decisions with regard to the sorting.

In connection with the sorting process, I repeat a statement made earlier in this paper: despite countless examples of conflict expressed in interviews, I believe there are three main categories under which most may be subsumed. These are (1) male-female, in particular the tension between husband and wife; (2) parent-child frictions, especially between male children and parents; and (3) frictions arising from a cluster of social class and social class related factors, mainly evident in disagreements between the family and the neighborhood or community, or between the husband and his employer.

Now the first task of the therapist is to seal the engagement, and the second is to assess pathogenic relating. In pursuing these tasks he explores the husband-wife relationship, and the parent-child relationship, and he tests the relationship of the family vis-à-vis community. He takes the role of the go-between when he acts as a facilitator of the information he desires. He also obtains important information when he takes sides with members against others or when he establishes a position on an issue vis-à-vis family members. Even as celebrant he obtains information that is needed by stating that he can only certify events or act as witness to them if he has the full details about them.

As go-between and as celebrant the therapist expresses certain values, but these are relatively fixed and limited in comparison to those he is able to express as side-taker. By definition as a side-taker he expresses values emphatically. In a husband-wife conflict he may throw his weight to the side of the husband *or* the wife. When he sides with the husband, characteristically he sides with those values I refer to as "discontinuity values," because in my experience husbands characteristically align themselves with these values vis-à-vis their wives, who characteristically align themselves with values I refer to as "continuity values." In a parent-child conflict the therapist may throw his weight to the side of the parents. When he does so he aligns himself with the "discontinuity values," because these are the ones characteristically espoused by parents in conflict with their children, who characteristically assert "continuity values." In a family-community conflict the therapist may throw his weight to the side of the community and thus express "discontinuity values," in contrast to those he would express if he sided with the family—namely, "continuity values."

Thus there is a commonality in the values expressed by *husbands* in conflict with wives, by *parents* in conflict with their children, and by the *community* in conflict with the family. Wives, children and families also share a set of values in conflicts with their husbands, parents and communities. The first commonality, the "discontinuity values," emphasizes the goodness of order, system, hierarchical arrangements or taxonomies, rules and procedures, analysis, selectivity and exclusivity. The second commonality, the "continuity values," deemphasizes order, system, hierarchical arrangements, etc., and stresses egalitarianism but mixed with an anti-uniformity. The unique incident, the special case—these are important "continuity values." By means of these commonalities, husbands and wives, parents and children, families and communities assert their identities, their wish to be useful and needed, their wish for affection or love, their desire for power and control and authority.

A common conflict between husbands and wives is disagreement over discipline of children. Typically it is the *husband* who accuses the *wife* of breaking the rules he thought existed (and which he may have devised more than she) regarding discipline. *He* accuses *her* of too much permissiveness, too much laxity. *She* accuses *him* of too much rigidity, too much severity. It is rather the same in conflicts between parents and children. Parents are accused of applying too many rules and procedures ("Be home before 9 p.m."). The children are defined as rule-breakers who always have a ready excuse. And in conflicts between the family and neighborhood or community, typically the family accuses the neighborhood or community of being too restrictive, of demanding too much in the way of regulation and conformity.

I have said before that the therapist is unavoidably caught up in side-taking. Because of the nature of the process in which he is engaged, he cannot avoid it; he can only try to capitalize on it rather than be victimized. As each issue expressed in interviews generates conflict, the therapist will hear the contending parties expressing the values I have referred to as "discontinuity values" and "continuity values," and he will be called on to join one side or the other. It makes a difference which side he joins, for by judicious side-taking the therapist can tip the balance against pathogenic relating. Does the family "need" or would it restore functioning in members for the therapist to espouse the "discontinuity values" of order, system, definition, rules, regulations, limits and boundaries? Does the family "need" or would it restore functioning in members for the therapist to espouse the "continuity values" of egalitarianism and the special case or unique incident?

I do not have a precise formula for the therapist to apply to moment-to-moment transactions in family interviews (for instance, one that would allow him to determine precisely with whom to side, at what moment and by what means), but I believe it will be a definite advantage to him to apply the guidelines I have suggested in this section. To review the guidelines briefly: (1) the three major categories of conflict observed in family interviews are (a) husband-wife, (b) parent-child, (c) family-community. (2) In the major conflicts, there is a commonality in the values expressed by husbands, parents and community versus those expressed by wives, children and family. (3) The commonality expressed by husbands, parents and community is labeled "discontinuity values;" whereas that expressed by wives, children and family is called "continuity values." (4) "Discontinuity values" express the goodness of order, system, definition, rules and regulations; whereas "continuity values" deemphasize order, system, definition, etc., while stressing egalitarianism, the special case and the unique incident. (5) As conflicts arise family members try to align the therapist with either the "discontinuity values" or "continuity values" they are expressing. (6) The therapist, *based on his diagnosis of pathogenic relating in the family*, can respond basically in two ways—he can espouse or throw his support to the "discontinuity values" or to the "continuity values." (7) The therapist's support for one set of values versus the other is not fixed, but can shift in response to the issues over which there is conflict.

Table 1 is an expansion of definitions cited earlier in this section for "continuity values" and "discontinuity values." Earlier, for example, "continuity values" were defined as those which deemphasized order, system, taxonomies, etc., and stressed egalitarianism mixed with anti-uniformity. This definition for "continuity values" is covered in two of the categories listed in Table 1: The moral/ethical and the cognitive/conceptual. Two other categories are added which provide more depth to the definitions of the

TABLE 1

Categories of Contrasting Values
Expressed in Family Interviews

Categories	Values	
	"Continuity"	"Discontinuity"
1. Affective/Attitudinal	Empathic Sympathetic "Warm"	Distant Reserved "Cool"
2. Moral/Ethical	Anticonformist Idealistic Egalitarian	Disciple of Law Order and Codes Pragmatic Elitist
3. Cognitive/Conceptual	Intuitive Holistic	Analytic Systematic
4. Tasks/Goals	Nurturing Caretaking	Achieving Structuring

contrasting values: these are the affective/attitudinal and tasks/goals. Along a dimension of affectivity, "continuity values" are expressed in empathy, sympathy or warmth; "discontinuity values" in distance, reserve, coolness. Along a dimension of orientation toward tasks or goals, "continuity values" are expressed by the act of nurturing or caretaking; "discontinuity values" by the impulse to achieve or structure.

TABLE 2

Contrasting Values Expressed by Various Conflicted Parties in Family Interviews

Conflict Between:	Values	
	"Continuity"	"Discontinuity"
1. Mates	Wife	Husband
2. Generations	Children	Parents
3a. Family and Community	Family	Community
3b. Family and Community—Race as a Central Factor	Black	White
3c. Family and Community—Social Class as a Central Factor	Lower Class	Middle Class
3d. Family and Community—Politics as a Central Factor	Liberal	Conservative

Table 2 is also an expansion and summarization of relationships described earlier in this section. Earlier it was stated that in conflict between mates, usually the husband espoused the "discontinuity values" vis-à-vis his wife who espoused the "continuity values." In conflict between generations, it was the parents who usually espoused the "discontinuity values" vis-à-vis children. In conflict between the family and community, usually the community espoused the "discontinuity values" vis-à-vis family. Table 2 elaborates several categories of the family-community conflict with respect to the contrasting set of values. For example, in family-community conflict centering on the issue of race, whites typically espouse the "discontinuity values" vis-à-vis blacks. In family-community conflicts centering on the issue of social class, the middle class typically espouses the "discontinuity values" vis-à-vis the lower class. And in family-community conflict centering on the issue of politics, typically conservatives espouse the "discontinuity values" as over against liberals.

CHAPTER 3

STYLE OF RELATING AS PATHOGENIC RELATING:
A FAMILY CASE STUDY

This is a report of a family I will call the Ashbys seen in therapy by me for three-and-one-half years (and continuing), in which all three offspring manifested psychiatric illness. The presenting problem was the youngest of the children, a preadolescent son who was exhibiting disturbed behavior in the classroom and at home. This youngster (we will call him Willy) was the subject of teasing by his classmates, to which he reacted by tears and temper tantrums. He was unusually tall for his age, which also caused him to "stick out like a sore thumb" at school. He was physically clumsy and spoke in a low, flat monotone. He was extremely intelligent for his age.

Willy's parents were also very intelligent. His father was a college professor, and during the course of therapy his mother completed a master's degree in library science. During the course of therapy she worked in various types of teaching jobs. Early on it was clear that the marriage did not provide much satisfaction. There had already been one lengthy separation, and the parents expressed discontent with each other. A sharp split between them occurred over the management of their oldest daughter, about 20 years old at the onset of therapy. Then out of the home on her own in a southern state, this girl became quite disturbed during her mid-teens and had already been hospitalized. She had left home in her late teens to travel on her own and make her way taking odd jobs and also working as a go-go dancer, much to the concern of her parents.

At onset of therapy, another son (we will call him Jed) was also residing at home. Jed was described as the most conformist of the children by the parents, perhaps less intelligent than the youngest son and the oldest girl, Melinda. Jed had just finished high school and was uncertain about his future vocation. He was not sure about college, so temporarily he took a job in carpentry.

The referral of the family for therapy was specifically because of the problem presented by Willy. Melinda was out of the home and therefore unavailable to attend interviews. Jed refused to attend interviews initially. During the second year of therapy he experienced a psychotic episode for which he was briefly hospitalized. Shortly after the hospitalization he agreed to attend interviews, and he attended intermittently since then. Also during the second year of therapy, Melinda was briefly hospitalized in a southern state for aberrant behavior, then was returned to Pennsylvania where her hospitalization was continued for a brief period of time before her psychosis resolved and she was accepted back home by her parents. (Her diagnosis in the hospital was paranoid schizophrenia.) Quite unexpectedly, Melinda agreed to participate in family interviews, and has been an irregular attender since. The frequency of interviews was as follows: about the first half-dozen with the family were weekly; the interval since then has been on a one every three- or four-week basis. The latter interval was one I thought the family could be comfortable with, whereas the former would, in my opinion, place too heavy demands upon the family for communication and exchange. Although there was a chronic state of family anxiety, frequent meetings were not the answer to reduce the anxiety. Frequent meetings may be counterproductive in that they put enormous demands on a family to relate, to communicate, and exchange—demands which may be totally inconsistent with the established style of relating. In the writer's opinion, therapists too frequently ignore this factor, and it is a major cause of premature termination.

The family therapy literature is deficient in reports on families seen as long as the Ashbys. The typical case is not seen nearly so long; rather the average case would be of a period of six months. But just because this is the length of the average case, long-term observation should not be ignored because only in the long term can certain types of family interaction be reliably observed as well as the effects of certain types of intervention assessed.

In this case it was possible, after the therapy had begun, to involve two children who were initially absent or reluctant to participate. There is a lack of research on the issue, but it is recognized among experienced therapists that it is difficult to involve family members who have not participated in the initial phase of therapy.

The parents were educated, articulate people who were concerned about their children and despaired about their condition. One striking feature about Willy, the youngest child for whom the family was referred, was the flat, toneless quality of his voice and the relative inexpressiveness of his eyes and other facial features. Both parents shared these characteristics with him. The voices of both were flat, controlled, while "nervous." Often I could not hear Mrs. Ashby and would ask her to speak up. Mr. Ashby's voice often quavered as if he were tense.

The flat, toneless, inexpressive quality noticed in the parents' voices and faces permeated their relationship with each other and the children. In time, I came to find both caring, feeling, concerned people, but there was little in their overt behavior with each other and the children that revealed this. To a remarkable extent, in overt behavior they matched the picture that Leo Kanner (1949) drew in the 1940s of typical parents of autistic children. Although Kanner recognized a so-called constitutional factor in autism, he was deeply impressed by the frequency with which the parents appeared cold, impersonal, and indifferent to their affected children.

In my lengthy contact with the Ashby parents, I came to discard the notion of malevolent motives in one or both as the basis for the pathogenic relating in the family. The notion of "bad" motives in individual members was not supported by my observations over three-and-one-half years, nor was the notion of a fixed family "type" whereby members enacted roles specified by the type, such as in the hypothetical "schizophrenogenic" family or "psychosomatogenic" family, with a specific mental illness (schizophrenic or psychosomatic) predicted by the family type. Although each of the children manifested mental illness, the characteristics and time of presentation of the illnesses differed in each.

It was only after about three years of contact with the Ashbys—after I had an opportunity to observe each of the Ashby children relate to each other and their parents in at least several interviews—that I gave credence to the notion that the parents' style of relating (their appearance of coolness, emotional flatness or blandness and impersonality) was indeed a significant causative factor in precipitating the pathogenic relating that led each of the children into a psychiatric illness. It is interesting that the illnesses manifested themselves somewhat differently in the children and at different points in their chronological development. Willy was nine years old when first seen in therapy, and my diagnostic impression was of a neurotic youngster marked by strong obsessive trends. A later diagnosis by another clinician called him "prepsychotic"—a diagnosis which may have some practical merit but which unfortunately begs the question of current mental status. When this latter diagnosis was made, Willy was a preadolescent of twelve years. Melinda, the daughter who was the oldest in the family, was first hospitalized at about age sixteen. The parents reported she had a psychotic episode. At age twenty, after having spent two years or more away from her family, she returned home after having been briefly hospitalized once again for psychotic behavior. Upon meeting Melinda, she impressed me as an intelligent girl, but emotionally immature and greatly lacking in self-confidence. She was preoccupied with herself, was without serious goals, and avoided close relationships. In sum, she impressed me as more of a borderline character disorder than a neurotic disorder. Jed, the middle child, had a first psychotic episode when about nineteen years of age, shortly after a number of disappointments with his job and girlfriend which caused him to become very anxious and depressed. He had also been experimenting with various drugs, although he later denied that drugs played any role in the mental confusion that led to his hospitalization. Twenty years old at the time this report is written, Jed is a reasonably intelligent young man, somewhat passive-dependent, not strongly goal-oriented, and might be classified neurotic with mild depression as a main symptom.

Although Willy reflected the parents' blandness of manner and verbal expression, and impersonality, neither Jed nor Melinda did. Both of them were more animated and emotionally responsive in interviews. The parents and Willy did indeed share a kind of schizoid quality as perceived in interviews, which Jed and Melinda did not. The parents' style of relating seemed to be a reflection of a set of values I have referred to (Zuk, 1979) as "discontinuity" values—which emphasize order, rationality, adherence to rules and regulations, require the maintenance of emotional distance and impersonality in decision-making, and so on. These values contrast with that set I have referred to as "continuity," which emphasize emotional responsiveness, closeness in human relations, egalitarianism, humanitarianism, and romanticism. Although it is more or less normal for parents to espouse "discontinuity" values in the parent-child relationship, the Ashbys' emphasis on this set of values was excessive, and was the object of challenge or assault by their children, although each challenge was unique and related to special qualities in each. Each child challenged the climate of "discontinuity" established by the parents, and each challenge evoked pathogenic relating which led each to manifest symptoms of a mental illness. I am not suggesting that the particular parent-child atmosphere of conflict was the *only* cause of the psychopathology, but rather that it was a significant and necessary contributor to the psychopathology, serving, as it were, as a trigger. I believe that children who feel deprived of the emotional intimacy that is the essence of the parent-child relationship, will react against the deprivation, seeking by so doing to restore it. Sometimes the reaction is excessive and violent, and the children manifest psychiatric illness or some other behavioral disorder or sociopathy. The Ashby case is intended to support this theory.

The type of family therapy conducted was the author's Go-Between Process (Zuk, 1975). The aim was to promote "continuity" values through the therapist's interventions as go-between, side-taker, and celebrant. In other words, the major goal of the therapist was to promote emotional expressiveness, warmth, and spontaneity, to encourage clear statements from family members of support and affection for each other, to be a sounding-board (as celebrant) of the succession of painful events that had beset the family, and serve as a clarion (again as celebrant) of a happier future in which parents and children would be more appropriately responsive to each other.

Case Study—The Ashbys

The following are the Ashby clinical notes with minor editing to respect anonymity, improve chronological continuity and clarity, and avoid unnecessary repetition.

Intake and Progress Note, Covering Period of January 27 through February 17, 1977

This is a mid-40s white Protestant couple with three children, the youngest 9 and oldest about 20. Father is a college professor; mother does substitute teaching. In the first meeting parents were accompanied by youngest son, Willy. He is the reason the family was referred by the school system. He appears a very bright but withdrawn youngster. Mother reports he is a problem at school and he does things to annoy her at home, such as refusing to obey or tearing up newspapers. The oldest child, a daughter of 20, has been a behavior problem for many years. Currently she is in a southern state, having left the family abruptly. This girl has already been hospitalized on the basis of what sounded like a psychotic episode. The middle child, a boy of 17, is living at home, is said to be "less bright" than the other two, more conformist. Parents had a rocky marriage the last few years. There was a separation of over one year recently. They have just gotten back together this past summer or fall. Both are quiet, controlled people who sort of "bottle up." There have been four meetings to date. The last three have been with the parents alone. I thought the presence of the youngster (Willy) would further bottle them up, but I will want to see him again and if possible his older brother. I am encouraging the parents to talk more openly.

Progress Note, Covering Period of February through June 23, 1977

There have been ten sessions in this period. The Ashbys have been very good about appearances for sessions, and seem to be deriving benefit. They appear more relaxed, and comment on better cooperation between parents, and a more positive attitude on Willy's part. Willy still feels that he is victimized by classmates, and I have worked with him to discourage this attitude. He gets very upset talking about the teasing that undoubtedly he is subjected to. His parents seem at a loss to offer him direction about this. I encourage them to come up with some helpful suggestions for him. Mr. Ashby talks with apprehension about his runaway daughter. I encourage him and wife to openly acknowledge their fears regarding the girl. At the same time I don't want to emphasize their guilt toward her. Their middle son is still at home and there is doubt about his course after leaving high school soon. He showed up at one session, but has not returned. My impression is that the parents have had a long-time difficulty with the problem of closeness—toward each other and the children. I think they are concerned and intelligent people, but have difficulty being emotionally receptive and affectionate. I think all of the kids have reacted against this "being held at a distance," and have punished the parents in their own way. I intend to continue with this interesting family, seeing them currently on an every-third-week basis.

Progress Note, Covering Period of July through December 16, 1977

There have been six meetings with the Ashbys in this period; in other words, we have been meeting about once per month. Progress seems maintained at an acceptable level. More recently there are reports from the parents that Willy's school behavior is improved, and his relationship with his older brother, Jed, is better on both sides. Mr. Ashby has returned to his teaching after a summer break and is experiencing what appear to be typical frustrations and annoyances in the new college term. Mrs. Ashby started back to college recently, is studying library science and hopes to take a master's degree. She is somewhat anxious about getting enough time to study to pass exams. I intend to continue with the family on about a once-a-month basis. On December 16 we "celebrated" our 20th interview.

Progress Note, Covering Period of December, 1977 through April 7, 1978

The Ashbys are seen about once monthly, and appear regularly. The most recent meeting was on April 7, and was the 23rd interview. Generally there is a favorable climate in the family. This is expressed most by Mr. Ashby, but his wife agrees. For one thing, Willy is getting better reports from teachers at school, and is less "pesty" at home. Jed got a job as a roofer but lost it, and is now doing odd jobs around the house for his parents. The parents say they are more helpful to each other. Mr. Ashby expresses this directly to his wife, and says he appreciates it very much. The most painful element in the family continues to be the condition of daughter Melinda, who was recently arrested on charges of vagrancy and solicitation. She called her parents to ask for help with attorney's fees. I have tried to focus on how the parents might better handle the stress produced by their daughter. One thing I suggested is that they limit the frequency and length of her telephone calls in which she is sure to recount her current plight and then ask for assistance, usually money. I tell them to limit the calls and specifically ask them *not* to go into details of her life because, since she appears to ignore their advice it makes them feel helpless and very anxious. Somewhat reluctantly, they agree to try to limit the telephone calls.

Progress Note, Covering Period of April through August 11, 1978

There have been four meetings in this period. In mid-May I inquired whether the Ashbys wanted to continue. I indicated what progress I thought had been made, and got their response about change they perceived. Both parents stated there had been substantial improvement in the family—and their marriage was more stable. Willy was much improved in the school setting and at home. Jed was taking more constructive steps vocationally and was more cooperative with his parents. The parents indicated they wanted to stay in touch with me on about a monthly basis and I agreed. After the interview in mid-May, there was a period of about three months before I heard from the Ashbys again. Apparently there was a feeling they would see if they could "go it alone" without the therapy. Then an entirely new and unexpected event brought them back into contact with me. Their daughter, Melinda, suddenly returned home. The story I got from Mr. Ashby was as follows: Melinda, who had been living in a southern state, decided she wanted to go to Boston and work there as a waitress and go-go dancer. She purchased an auto and started the drive north. On the way she claims her auto was stolen. When the police investigated, they became concerned by her incoherency and she was placed in a state psychiatric institution, where she remained for two months. She then left the hospital without permission and, with money provided by her father, flew to the Philadelphia area where it was recommended to her father that she be hospitalized—and she was in a psychiatric ward of a suburban general hospital. Melinda improved and stabilized in the hospital and was released after a few weeks to her parents. I encouraged the parents to bring her to family interviews, and I first saw her on August 8 and again on August 11. She is an intelligent young woman, not unattractive, although careless in personal appearance. In retelling recent events, there were hints that she embellished the story, and she revealed a very suspicious attitude toward the civil authorities with whom she became involved, such as the police. It seemed clear she carried deep resentment toward her parents. At one point in the session on August 11, after some prodding from me, Melinda burst into tears, bitterly assailing her parents. She shouted she would never let them "use" her as they had in the past, and I asked what this meant. She said they had used her illness or bad behavior as an excuse to avoid dealing with the problem in their marriage. I told Melinda that, although this was probably true in the past, I thought her parents were making genuine efforts to help themselves and the family, and added she had an obligation to them as a daughter to test their good will. I asked her to give it six months (that is, to stay home for six months and participate in therapy) in order to see if they had really changed and whether her attitude toward them could change.

Progress Note, Covering Period of August through December 15, 1978

Ten meetings are covered in this note. Melinda has participated in almost all. She is making satisfactory adjustment at home, has started college courses, and is not seriously provoking parental anxieties. I believe she has stopped using psychotropic medication that had been prescribed. She appears nervous in meetings, but communicates, if sparingly. She obviously doesn't want to get involved in "heavy" conversation in meetings. A major event producing disturbance in the family in this period was the brief hospitalization of Jed, 19, who had become increasingly "hyper," according to his parents, during November. He created a disturbance during a meeting at a nearby college and was admitted to the psychiatric ward of a nearby general hospital. He verbalized some unusual ideas to the police and his parents and others—the reaction sounded like a psychotic episode. Jed had had some hurtful things happening to him just prior to the episode: his girlfriend found another boyfriend; he was fired from his job; and one or two other distressing incidents. Later he said, when I asked him, that he had not been taking drugs; he insisted, in other words, that drugs were unrelated to the psychotic episode. In the 37th interview with the family, held on December 15, 1978, Jed actually showed up. (With one exception he had consistently refused to attend before.) He was in reasonably good touch, but still slightly "hyper." For example, he said he was continuing to take lithium—prescribed for him by the psychiatrist who saw him while hospitalized—but had declined to continue another drug because it would interfere with his "libido." Melinda appeared to be holding her own during the crisis presented by Jed. Mr. and Mrs. Ashby were trying hard to maintain their equilibrium in the face of the very upsetting experience with Jed. According to his parents, Willy was being cooperative.

Progress Note, Covering Period of December, 1978 through April 5, 1979

In this period there have been four sessions. In most all family members have appeared; except Melinda was absent for one or two. Things appear stable. Jed has been asymptomatic, and has started taking courses at a nearby college. Melinda is taking a pretty full course load at college. She "threatened" to go back to go-go dancing a few weeks ago in order to earn money, but apparently this threat evaporated—at least for the time being. She is relatively symptom-free and reported a loss of 15 pounds. The weight loss may be a response to the attentions of a new boyfriend. Physically she looks better. Willy has had a couple of temper tantrums at school, to which the school has responded by instituting a system of "negative reinforcement" along behaviorist lines—and he has responded more or less positively. Mr. Ashby is worried about paying bills. Now he is paying for the schooling of all three children and is financially strapped. Mrs. Ashby is currently doing part-time work as a substitute teacher. In the most recent session, she looked more physically composed than I have seen her in the past. Although worried about bills, Mr. Ashby conveyed in the most recent meeting a greater sense of control in dealing with family affairs.

Progress Note, Covering Period of April through October 10, 1979

This note covers six sessions with the family in about a five-month period. In the two most recent sessions all family members have been present. Melinda did not appear for three of the meetings. During part of the summer she left home for the Midwest to work clubs as a go-go dancer. The parents were anxious about her but also relieved that she was out of the house. I told them I thought that Melinda was threatening them badly and they deserved better from her, and that they should *demand* better if she returned home. In September she did return, but continued her distant attitude toward her parents. In sessions she then attended, I confronted her strongly on her bad treatment of her parents, to the point where she burst into tears, insisting that she was trying to relate to them in a warmer fashion. I said I thought she wasn't trying hard enough to do so; that her parents deserved more from her and did not warrant her contempt at this time in their lives. Jed seems to be faring nicely. He is back working as a roofer, but has also started taking college courses. Upon return from her sojourn in the Midwest, Melinda also is taking several college courses this fall. Jed seems settled down from his hypomanic state. Mr. and Mrs. Ashby are bearing the strains of parenting with equanimity, but I have suggested there are times with children when equanimity may not be desirable. I was saying, in other words, that there are times with children when to be "cool" creates a climate of uncertainty and distance and is harmful. I suggested they set out more definite guidelines for the behavior of the children, and that they were entitled to insist that the guidelines be honored. Willy encountered difficulty handling a summer camp experience. Upon his return home from camp I suggested to his parents that they explore individual psychotherapy for Willy, for he was anxious and excitable in interviews, and I was concerned about his mental status. I thought it might be helpful for him to have a course of individual psychotherapy—a person he could unburden himself to—and recommended this to his parents. In the fall he started regular public school after having been in a private school for several years, and I was concerned how he would react to the new classroom situation.

Progress Note, Covering Period of October, 1979 through February 29, 1980

Four interviews are covered in this note. Early in November, Willy was booted out of public school. A psychiatric evaluation was made by the school system and he was labeled "pre-psychotic" with a recommendation for placement in a special classroom for emotionally disturbed children. Such a placement was obtained. This episode was a crisis to which the parents responded with considerable anxiety. I worked with them to try to put the situation in some perspective. In particular I played down the psychiatric diagnosis that was communicated to them, and to some extent disassociated myself from it, although I concurred with the suggestion for special school placement. Melinda added to the parents' trials during this period. She was taking jobs as a go-go dancer and dropped her college courses. Jed also dropped a plan to resume college courses, but was working as a laborer. Mr. and Mrs. Ashby were barely holding their own through this period. One feels sympathy for these parents. They have convinced me of their sincerity in wanting to help their children. They have enormous difficulty in *expressing* this concern to their children, and it must be a difficulty of long standing. The two older children show continued resentment against their parents for what they feel was lack of concern during their earlier years. They cannot forgive them for this "injury," and punish them for it severely.

Progress Note, Covering Period of March through June 27, 1980

Four meetings are covered in this note. It was a period of recovery from the crisis and anxiety described in the previous note. Willy, after a shaky start, made a good adjustment at the special school to which he was sent. The interview held on June 27 was the 55th with the family. Melinda was not present. She accompanied her parents when the family went on a brief holiday to the New Jersey seashore, and apparently enjoyed herself. She has begun to talk about returning to college again. In interview No. 55 Mrs. Ashby and her husband seemed in a lighter mood, and even Willy was lighthearted. Willy thinks his teachers are "nice" (he repeated this assessment again from the previous session). Willy was neatly dressed in the 55th session, something not typical for him in the past. His speech was more animated; he was more alert. He talked with pleasure about operating a new home computer his father has purchased. Mrs. Ashby has received her master's degree in library science and is obviously pleased. Her husband bought her a nice gift for her graduation. The parents are planning a vacation but diverge on where to go. I tell them this is a problem they can work on and solve together—that it will be good exercise for them to work it out. Jed continued to be employed. Mr. Ashby is worried that he seems to drink a lot of beer, but Mrs. Ashby thinks it is not such a great quantity as her husband suggests and is not bothered.

Summary

This formal case report is believed justified for the following reasons:

1. The case provides evidence based on an extended clinical contact that *style of relating* in parents is an important component of pathogenic relating leading to psychiatric illness in children, who are at risk because of their dependent role in the relationship.

2. The case suggests a definition for style of relating in a family *as a selection and promotion of certain values over others*; in the case of the Ashbys, the selection made by the parents was a systematic application of "discontinuity" over "continuity" values.

3. The writer ruled out bad or malevolent motives toward the children as causal elements in the psychopathology on the basis of his clinical contact over a three-and-one-half-year period.

4. The writer did conclude that the parents' impersonal, emotionally distant style of relating was a likely causal agent leading to the eventual manifestation in each of their children of a psychiatric illness.

5. All three children manifested psychiatric illness, although differing in kind and point of onset during adolescence and preadolescence. Neither of the parents—although both were perceptibly depressed at times—clearly manifested a mental illness.

6. The risk of manifest mental illness is greater in children than parents who exhibit an impersonal style of relating *because the children are in the more dependent position, and because the emotional intimacy inherent in the parent-child relationship requires children to challenge impersonality*.

7. The family therapy literature is short on cases seen for as long as the Ashbys. Although the majority of family therapy cases are seen for a relatively brief time (six months or less), and short-term methods are most practical, it is important to report long-term cases also because only in the long-term can certain family processes be reliably and accurately assessed, as well as the effect of certain interventions of a therapeutic nature.

8. Two of the Ashby children were either unavailable or unwilling to participate in therapy at the beginning, but after it was possible to involve both,

even if on an irregular basis. Experienced therapists are aware that it is especially difficult to engage family members who are not present at initial interviews, so the Ashby case was an exception to this rule. The presence of a crisis just preceding their involvement undoubtedly facilitated their involvement.

9. The therapy, conducted along the lines of the Go-Between Process, served somewhat to normalize and stabilize the behavior of the children, and the parents reported that their marriage was more cooperative. The major objective of the therapy was to introduce and promote "continuity" values to offset the destructive effects of a long-time imbalance in favor of "discontinuity" values practiced by the parents toward each other and the children.

10. Style of relating should be a major dimension in typologies attempting to discriminate family function or dysfunction. In such typologies, more emphasis should be placed on values as *dynamic* components.

CHAPTER 4

ORDINARY PEOPLE AND THE TRUNCATED NUCLEAR FAMILY

In the past two years two motion pictures have struck a special chord in audiences in the United States. The films are *Kramer vs. Kramer* and *Ordinary People*. One notices that audiences leaving theaters at which they are playing are quiet, and one sees many tearful people. The interest in these movies extends outside the United States, although they both represent situations especially prevalent in the United States. Last year while on a speaking engagement in Argentina, I was asked numerous times what I thought of *Kramer vs. Kramer*. I had to confess I hadn't seen it, although I made it my business to do so in Buenos Aires. Recently my wife, a child psychiatrist, and I saw *Ordinary People*.

Both films portray families that are variants of what I have called the "truncated" nuclear family. These are nuclear families—meaning families restricted to two generations usually living in the same household, ordinarily signifying parents and their children—in which, sometimes due to the stress of change in life cycle of members, sometimes to accidental or unexpected events that produce crisis, values are polarized between the spouses or between parents and their children, thus setting the stage for what I have called pathogenic relating. Pathogenic relating refers to subtle or not so subtle forms of intimidation and threat. A subtle form might be silencing, in which family members act in concert to silence another as a form of discipline or punishment. A direct form would be verbal threat or outright physical assault, as in the case of wife or child abuse. Pathogenic relating sets the stage for disorganized behavior and psychiatric illness.

Kramer vs. Kramer is a movie about a phenomenon that has only recently become significant in terms of American population statistics— the "runaway wife" phenomenon in which custody of the children is left with the husband. *Ordinary People* is about a phenomenon that has been very prevalent in the United States since the end of World War II—the educated, upper middle-class suburban family in which husband, wife, and children occupy the same household but are estranged from one another.

In its garden-variety form, the truncated nuclear family is one in which the husband-father has become a peripheral figure or is absent from wife and children, who form a tightly knit core, sharing values espoused by the wife-mother. The husband-father's absence has been brought about by the demands of the workplace, and his tendency to bring the business ethic into the home where, if applied with too heavy a hand, the ethic will collide with other values that are common to family relationships. The business or workplace ethic is included in a set of values I have called "discontinuity" values, which place a premium on orderly, rational conduct, on rules and regulations, on being objective or maintaining emotional distance when trying to solve problems. It contrasts with "continuity" values, which place a premium on emotional closeness and permissiveness, on egalitarianism as opposed to elitism, and on intuition as opposed to rational analysis.

In the nuclear family it is the typical case that the wife-mother is the major exponent of "continuity" values, the husband-father of "discontinuity" values. In the stable marriage, these values blend or are in balance and there is harmony. The truncated nuclear family describes a family in which the values are not in balance and there is disharmony. In the stable nuclear family, the parents tend to be the main exponents of "discontinuity" values vis-à-vis children, who espouse "continuity" values. In the truncated nuclear family, the main focus of conflict may be between parents and children, and one may see values sharply polarized between these parties. In the common form of truncated nuclear family, a collision of values exists between the spouses and also between spouses and children. The children are at special risk because theirs is the most dependent position in the family. If they ally too closely with their mother and the "continuity" values she is most likely to espouse, then they become hostile to their father and the "discontinuity" values he is most likely to espouse. The time of greatest risk to the children is at the point of leaving the family, because the outside community they are attempting to join is, like the father, a major exponent of "discontinuity" values.

The Family in *Ordinary People*

Ordinary People is about a variant of the truncated nuclear family. In this the wife-mother struggles to outdo her husband in bringing the business ethic ("discontinuity" values) into the home. She runs a "tight ship"—everything neat, clean, in its proper place. It works well up to a point: it shows itself inadequate in the face of severe life crisis.

The story of *Ordinary People* is about a teenager who returns home following a stay at a mental hospital precipitated by a suicide attempt. Apparently the attempt was triggered by a recent episode in which, while sailing, the boy and his older brother are caught in a storm and the older brother is drowned. The boy has nightmares of the drowning and severe anxiety attacks.

His parents—young middle-aged, attractive, well-educated suburbanites—are worried about him. They are not sure to what extent he has recovered; that is, to what extent he will not trouble them again by repeating an effort at suicide. His father is saddened, puzzled at what to do for his son. His mother is trying to be tolerant of him, but gets angry when her attempts to show concern are rejected.

The boy returns to his high school and tries to blend in, but something is missing. He is distracted, finds he cannot participate, cannot share the interests of his peers. He continues to be haunted by nightmares. His father suggests he visit a psychiatrist, but at first the boy resists the idea. He should be able to pull himself out of his situation by will and determination. Finally he feels compelled to make an appointment.

The boy initiates contact with a girl he has known at high school who was at the mental hospital as a patient the same time he was. He communicates his uneasiness to her, but she is unresponsive. She tells him to forget the past, live as if the hospital experience didn't happen.

His mother finds the boy alone in the backyard of their home. She feels she ought to try to communicate with him. She tells him he ought to be wearing a coat against the brisk fall weather. They try to talk, but they cannot. The boy is upset by what he feels is his mother's phony effort to communicate. She reminds him again to put on a coat and walks quickly away.

The parents are driving to a dinner party. The husband doesn't want to attend and suggests that instead he and his wife go to a movie. The wife seems to go along at first, but then reminds him that they would have a lame excuse for the hosts, and they drive on to the party. They enter into the lighthearted spirit of the participants, relating casually, cleverly. Later the husband encounters a woman acquaintance who asks about his son, and he replies that the boy is feeling great. She expresses sympathy, and the father finds himself revealing the fact that the boy is seeing a psychiatrist. His wife overhears this admission and interrupts and changes the conversation. Driving home, the wife is furious at her husband for revealing the "secret." Why? Because it is a breach of family confidence.

The extent of the gap between wife and son is becoming apparent to the husband. He decides to visit the son's psychiatrist, ostensibly to learn about his son's status, but then he admits he is troubled and may need a "shrink" himself. He says he cannot understand his wife's attitude. He knows she favored the older son, but in many respects she and the younger son are more alike. He recalls to the psychiatrist a scene with his wife just before they left for the older son's funeral. She insisted that he change his shirt and shoes. He was amazed that she could be concerned about the shirt and shoes at a moment of such grief. At home later, he reminds his wife directly about this incident, but she refuses to explain, saying that it is best not to dig up the past.

The wife decides that she and her husband really need to get away from the stress at home, and suggests a visit to her brother and sister-in-law in Houston. Her husband agrees and they leave by plane in an easy frame of mind. They are seen on the golf course and are enjoying themselves until her husband passes a remark about their son. She flares up at him, attracting the attention of bystanders. What should she do—tear herself into pieces? What do other mothers do? How is one supposed to act with a boy like hers?

While his parents are in Houston, the boy has a date with a vivacious girl with whom he sings at church choir. She has flirted with him, and he is attracted to her. At an eating place their conversation is interrupted by a group of rowdy young boys, and the girl joins in the "fun" to the consternation of her date. He drives her home in silence and, increasingly disturbed, returns to his home. He decides to place a phone call to Karen, the girl with whom he shared the experience at the state hospital. He reaches her parents, and is informed that Karen has committed suicide. He becomes panicky upon hearing this news, and the thought of suicide crosses his mind. He phones his psychiatrist, who agrees to meet him for a late night appointment. With his psychiatrist he blurts out his belief that he is responsible for his brother's death—just as if he had killed him himself, and that his mother's hatred of him is therefore justified. The psychiatrist asserts that the boy is not responsible for what happened to his brother, that it was beyond his control, and asks if he can forgive his mother for not having enough capacity to love him as much as his brother. Accepting the psychiatrist's wisdom and personal support, the boy embraces him.

The parents have returned home, and the son meets them in the living room of the house. He approaches his mother, embraces her and tells her that he loves her. She is dumbstruck, speechless. Later at night, she awakes to find her husband absent from the bedroom, and she looks for him downstairs. She finds him crying and asks why. He says it is because he realizes he doesn't know her, and the discovery saddens and frightens him. He is not sure now that he can love her. Profoundly injured by these remarks, the wife packs her bags and leaves the house to return to her brother in Houston.

Early in the morning the son spies his father in the backyard and having seen his mother leave in a taxi, asks where she went. The father replies simply that she has gone away for a while. Sensing the parental separation, the son immediately blames himself for it, but with intensity his father says it isn't his fault. Father and son look at one another and embrace.

Therapy for the Truncated Nuclear Family

All appears to have gone well in the family depicted in *Ordinary People* until a shocking event happens to one of the members. The family undergoes a severe test, a test of its values. But it is weak in precisely those values which are crucial at such times, namely "continuity" values which emphasize emotional nurturance. The values which work so well in the marketplace, "discontinuity" values, even in crises in the marketplace, are inadequate to deal with severe family crisis.

The American public was shocked to learn that the Hinckley youth, charged in the assassination attempt on the life of President Reagan on the afternoon of March 30, 1981, came from a "good" family. I have no direct knowledge about the Hinckley family, but *Ordinary People* conveys brilliantly a family type and circumstances which can lead a member to commit desperate acts against himself or others.

The boy in *Ordinary People* was spared, in my judgment, by three timely interventions: (1) the attention of a skilled mental health practitioner; (2) the boost to his self-esteem by a vivacious young woman; and (3) the gradual awakening of the father to fully support his son in the face of his wife's objections. The father was in what I have called a "go-between" role between wife and son, but tilting somewhat toward the position of his wife. When he makes his painful discovery, he reverses the tilt in the direction of his son, siding, so to speak, with his son against his wife. The change is important to his son's recovery, but costs the husband his wife.

A course of family therapy was suggested by the psychiatrist to the husband, but his wife rejects the idea. In my judgment, family therapy is the treatment of choice for the variant form of truncated family depicted in *Ordinary People*, but one limitation is that members may not be ready to undertake the stress. In the movie individual therapy was effective—it helped the boy, but at the expense of the marriage. A special strength of family therapy is that it reduces the risk of such side effects.

In family therapy, in the many issues that arise, therapist and family members interact mainly in what I believe to be three roles, which I have defined as those of the "go-between," "side-taker," and "celebrant." These occur outside of the therapy situation also. Above I referred to how the husband played the go-between vis-à-vis wife and son, and also how he was obligated to be a side-taker on behalf of his son when he made his discovery about his wife. The celebrant role is a very special one. In the movie it is enacted when the psychiatrist hears the boy's confession about his brother and then seeks to absolve the boy from guilt. So while the celebrant role is particularly applicable to family therapy, it can occur also in individual therapy.

The price paid by the nuclear family for its dominance in American family life during the past four decades is reflected in what are very large numbers indeed of truncated nuclear families. We have some indicators of large numbers in current statistics on separation and divorce, mental illness, delinquency and crimes by young adults, and wife and child abuse. These statistics are generally considered to be alarmingly high. There are less ominous but no less compelling statistics reflecting the incidence of truncated nuclear families. In 1979 there were reported to be nearly eight-and-one-half million families headed by a woman, the majority of these falling into the category commonly referred to as the single parent family, ordinarily composed of a woman providing for her children. A recent nationwide study found that more than five women out of ten living in families are now employed outside the home; only three out of ten women today are full-time homemakers. Most women working outside the home are married and have children under age 18 at home.

What the statistics say and have been saying is that not only has the marketplace provided the basis for the nuclear family's dominance in American society and Western societies generally, but the marketplace has also helped determine how the nuclear family has been inadequate to meet its continuing demands. The marketplace and an advancing technology that supports it have helped create the dominance of the nuclear family, which is a family form that encourages individual initiative and achievement, thereby serving the needs of the marketplace. But a heavy toll has been taken on those families that have not been quite ready for the independent status that is the hallmark of the nuclear family, or that have experienced unexpected or unusual events that have impaired their readiness to perform independently.

During the 19th century in Western societies, mental illness was believed caused mainly by hereditary factors or physical trauma. Sigmund Freud altered that view in the late 19th and early 20th centuries by persuasively presenting the case that certain childhood events produced emotional trauma that persisted in an unconscious trace into adulthood, and that this was a major cause of mental illness. Toward the middle of the 20th century such brilliant revisionists as Harry Stack Sullivan and Erik Erikson proposed that adolescence was an especially critical period, and that incompleted tasks associated with adolescence could later trigger mental illness. The family became a focus of attention as a possible causal source during the 1960s and 1970s. Proponents argued that the structure and function of the family could dispose members toward mental stability or illness.

In my judgment the family theorists have not taken sufficient account of the stress of the marketplace and technology on families, and to some extent have also been deficient in considering the impact of cultural inheritance (ethnic, racial, religious factors, for instance). I look for greater attention being paid to these factors in the future. Causation of mental illness by dysfunction in family interaction or relationships is the subject of intense investigation in psychiatric research today, and is generally conceded one of the strongest trends in mental health. While few mental health experts would agree that dysfunctional family relationships are the sole cause of mental illness, a majority today would agree on the family unit as a major source of mental well-being or disturbance. The family unit refers to the totality of relationships in the family, to the culture of the family, to those accidental or unexpected events that affect every family, and to the manner in which the family orients itself to the demands of the marketplace and technology.

Using the powerful medium of filmed drama, *Ordinary People* is superior to the clinical case study or empirical research as a truthful commentary on the plight of the modern family in the United States.

CHAPTER 5

TOWARD A VALUE DIFFUSION THEORY OF DEPRESSION

In discussions of depression in a recent major psychiatric text (Klerman, 1980; Wolpert, 1980), four theories are prominent: (1) the psychodynamic, almost exclusively psychoanalytic; (2) the hereditary, which includes constitution as a factor; (3) the biological or neurochemical; and (4) the behavioral or learning theory, which is strongly environmentalistic (e.g., Seligman's "learned helplessness"). For the purposes of this article, which emphasizes psychological theories of depression, only the psychodynamic and to some extent the behavior theories will be explicated.

Psychodynamic theory is split into three parts or stages. Perhaps the earliest is Abraham's (1927) formulation that depression was the result of loss of a loved object (person), and loss produced a regression to an infantile state (the oral-sadistic) in which separation from or loss of the mother caused trauma. Spitz (1946) and Bowlby (1969) evolved the work of Abraham in their studies of anaclitic depression.

The second stage of psychodynamic theory of depression is exemplified by the work of Fenichel (1945), who considered the major loss to be self-esteem. For the depressive, the world was barren and meaningless, and one did not deserve to have goals satisfied. Bibring (1953) viewed the source of the lost self-esteem as a regression to a trauma of early childhood, occurring in the anal or phallic phases. Trauma at these stages left one with a continuing anxiety that one could not master one's own body or the environment, or live up to one's own or others' expectations. Blatt (1974) refers to this type as introjective depression. It originates at a later stage of ego development than anaclitic depression.

The work of Arieti and Bemporad (1980) typifies the third stage of the psychodynamic theory. Focusing on family structure, these authors suggest from clinical studies that depressives have parents that demanded conformity and/or adherence to high ideals. In the very young child, failure to conform was met by threats of parental abandonment. In later childhood, the failure to live up to high ideals induced the parents to cause the child to feel guilty or ashamed. In adulthood, depression was caused by the loss of an object (person) on whom one depended, or by loss of or failure to achieve a desired goal. Both types of loss evoked the childhood trauma of rejection by the parents. Arieti and Bemporad refer to the first type of loss as the Dominant Other, and the second as the Dominant Goal.

One might expect a cognitive theory of depression, essentially based on behavior or learning theory, not to utilize concepts from psychodynamic theory, but such is not the case with Beck's theory (1983). Beck acknowledges a debt to Bowlby's work on anaclitic depression, and originally considered all depression as due to loss of a needed dependency relationship. But he found that not all cases fit this explanation—in some cases, the loss was of the individual's autonomy or sense of individuality. He has adapted his cognitive therapy to both these types of depression. For the first type, he stresses the therapist's need to develop a more personal relationship with the patient; for the second, the accent is on problem solving—the patient is taught to be active and achieve goals that he or she thought previously impossible to achieve.

Perhaps the most orthodox of the behavioral or learning theories of depression is Seligman's (1974) learned helplessness theory. Learned helplessness is incorporated as a role in bits and pieces over time by accumulation of experiences of failing, of feeling worthless because one has failed, of being unable to make decisions, of feeling isolated from others, of becoming passive and uncompetitive. Learned helplessness, Seligman argues, is the analogue for clinical depression. Learning helplessness may take place in childhood, but may also occur at any stage in life. Like psychodynamic theory, this theory accepts that a *loss* in adulthood characteristically triggers clinical depression, but unlike psychodynamic theory it does not posit that the adult loss evokes a trauma involving loss experienced only in infancy or early childhood.

Value Diffusion Theory

Here I will describe the value diffusion theory of depression, comparing and contrasting it with the two major psychological theories that have been described above. The article will also provide a case study of a depressed elderly woman to illustrate value diffusion theory.

Value diffusion theory agrees with psychodynamic theory in accepting the notion of loss as a critical factor inducing depression, but considers loss to be more a trigger to destabilize values than an analogue for loss experienced in infancy or early childhood. Like psychodynamic theory, value diffusion theory acknowledges two types of losses that are especially critical for the onset of depression: the loss of an object (person) on whom one has become very dependent, and the loss of or failure to achieve a desired goal. But unlike psychodynamic theory, value diffusion theory considers that these two types of losses reflect fundamental *values* that have come to form an essential core of the character of a person. Dependency is what I have referred to (Zuk, 1981a) as a "continuity" value, and goal achievement is what I have called a "discontinuity" value.

Like behavioral or learning theory, value diffusion theory accepts the notion that depression is not caused by trauma occurring at one moment in infancy or early childhood in the life cycle, but that each stage in the life cycle may contribute to causation *because values change and may be added or lost throughout the life cycle.* Unlike behavioral or learning theory, value diffusion theory states that a sudden or gradual destabilization of values that form an essential part of the character of a person is the root cause of depression, and not the cumulative effect of learning that one is a failure.

Reference has been made to "continuity" and "discontinuity" values that characterize persons, and I would like to present a table of mine (Zuk, 1981a, p. 241) that defines and contrasts these value sets. These sets are derived from more than 20 years of experience studying marital and family conflict. Several years ago it occurred to me that marital and family conflict (which was expressed in literally hundreds of issues) could almost always be reduced to a value conflict, and that between husbands and wives, parents and children, and family and community (the three major parties in conflict), commonly two sets of conflicting values could be discerned—and these I came to call the "continuity" and the "discontinuity." In husband-wife conflict, commonly the wife espoused "continuity" values, the husband "discontinuity." In parent-child conflict, commonly the children espoused the "continuity" values, the parents "discontinuity." And in family-community conflicts, commonly the family espouses "continuity" values, the community "discontinuity." Of course there were numerous exceptions to these rules, and numerous variations, as seems universally the case with respect to human relationships.

Table 2 is an attempt (Zuk, 1981a, p. 249) to relate the value sets to clinical psychopathology, but it should be noted that depression is not among the clinical entities listed. Table 2 suggests a specific relationship between values and individual psychiatric disturbance. Table 1 provides a paradigm to understand conflict between or among individuals, not within an individual, which is suggested—at least from the perspective of psychopathology—in Table 2.

Table 3 is an attempt to correlate the value systems with a clinical entity missing from Table 2, namely, depression. More specifically, it attempts to integrate the value systems according to the psychodynamic theory of depression described earlier, and also according to Beck's cognitive concept of depression.

Value diffusion theory defines depression as the mental state produced by, first, the destabilization and, second, the diffusion of the core of "continuity-discontinuity" values that personify a particular individual. Destabilization is the state most often produced in an individual by a perceived loss of a valued relationship, role, or goal; it is a necessary but not sufficient cause of depres-

TABLE 1

Categories of Values Expressed in Family Conflict

Categories	Values	
	"Continuity"	"Discontinuity"
Affective/Attitudinal	Empathic, Sympathetic	Distant, Reserved, "Cool"
Moral/Ethical	Idealistic, Egalitarian, Anticonformist	Disciple of Law and Codes, Pragmatic, Elitist
Cognitive/Perceptual	Intuitive, Holistic	Analytic, Systematic
Tasks/Goals	Nurturing, Caretaking	Achieving, Structuring

sion. It and not loss is the precondition, insofar as the theory is concerned, for value diffusion, which refers to a rupture in the configuration of "continuity-discontinuity" values. Depression is a result of the rupture or diffusion of values; it follows because the individual has actually experienced a loss of identity or self.

But why is depression rather than some other major mental disorder the typi-

TABLE 2

Value Systems in Relation to Psychiatric Nosology

Psychiatric Disorder	Values	
	"Continuity"	"Discontinuity"
Neurotic Level	Conduct Disorders	Psychosomatic
Characterologic Level	Hysteric	Obsessive-Compulsive
Psychotic Level	Catatonic or Hebephrenic	Paranoid

TABLE 3

Relation between Psychodynamic and Cognitive Concepts and Value Diffusion Theory

Depression Theories and Theorists	Values Underlying Value Diffusion Theory	
	"Continuity"	"Discontinuity"
Psychodynamic: Abraham, Fenichel, Bibring, Spitz, Bowlby, and others	Anaclitic Depression	Introjective Depression
Arieti and Bemporad	Dominant Other	Dominant Goal
Cognitive-Behavioral: Beck	Socially Dependent (Sociality)	Achievement Oriented (Autonomous)

cal result of value diffusion? Value diffusion theory would suggest that depression is the most likely result because it is the state from which *recovery* is most likely; in other words, it has survival value, in the Darwinian sense. Klerman (1980) specifically cites the adaptive function of depression and comments extensively on "depression as a normal human emotion" (p. 1306). It is known that there is a higher prevalence and also a higher spontaneous recovery rate in depression than other major mental illnesses, and that prognosis generally is better than for other major disorders (Wolpert, 1980).

Case Study

Mrs. R is a Jewish woman, almost 70 years old, who was born and reared in the South. She has several grown children who live near her. After the death of her husband three years ago, Mrs. R chose to live by herself. Her children noted that her depressions started approximately ten years ago, which would have been a year or two after her mother died at 83 years of age. Mrs. R was apparently very close to her mother, and nursed her during her last years. During the few years after her mother's death, she saw several psychiatrists who prescribed medications, and even tried electroshock. These means had some success and she was able to maintain herself outside the hospital until 1975, when she had a severe depressive episode that required her hospitalization for a relatively brief period.

She did reasonably well until about two years after her husband died in 1979, when she again experienced a severe depressive episode that required her hospitalization for approximately three months. She did well in the hospital and when she left told her children that she felt "on top of the world." She arranged a number of visits to friends and relatives and carried them out successfully. But then things turned sour when she returned home to find—so she claims—errors made by her accountant in preparing income tax returns. She became increasingly disturbed, feeling that she had paid too much money to the government. Quickly she fell into another depression and was hospitalized a third time. Again she did well in the hospital on a combination of antidepressants—an antipsychotic had also been used—lithium, milieu therapy, individual psychotherapy, and family interviews conducted by this author.

In the two family interviews conducted while Mrs. R was in the hospital just prior to her release, I met her and most of her grown children. I learned that her husband had been a hard-driving, ambitious man on whom she was quite dependent, but she resented that he was often away on business and she was left alone to care for the children. She felt that she was a dutiful wife and mother who actively participated in community affairs as befitted a woman of her social and economic standing. Her children claimed that while they loved their mother, they never felt very close to her. They thought that she felt that they had failed her in not living up to the high standards set by their father. They lacked the ambition, drive, and aggressiveness that he seemed to have had in ample quantity.

In the family interview conducted just before she was released, Mrs. R announced that she had made a good friend while in the hospital and wished that this friend, a younger woman also hospitalized for a depressive episode, would come to live with her and share her home, and they would plan activities together and do some traveling. Watching the faces of her children while she was reporting this, it was clear to me that they were alarmed at the prospect. They didn't seem to like the idea of anyone getting between them and their mother even though they had felt for a long time that she had rejected them. I thought it was possible that they feared the possible effect of this new friend on their potential inheritance.

The next time I met Mrs. R and family was about six weeks after she left the hospital. The psychiatric resident who had followed her in the hospital and on an outpatient basis was concerned that her mental status had deteriorated, and asked for a consultation. Mrs. R and her children seemed glad enough to see me. I asked about her friend—whether she had come to live with Mrs. R as planned—and was told by Mrs. R that no, it didn't happen, and I didn't wish to pursue the matter further in the context of the family interview. She told me that she had returned to her apartment (she moved from their long-occupied home to an apartment sometime after her husband died), did not leave it much except to make some purchases, made the simplest meals for herself (usually frozen prepared meals), tired easily, and looked forward to bedtime and sleep. She appeared physically to be somewhat sad but not clearly depressed, slightly preoccupied, but related to me directly and rationally.

I asked Mrs. R's children how she appeared to them and immediately received statements of alarm and complaint. They tried, they said, to engage her in family activities, but she just wasn't interested and usually declined. When she did attend, she complained about her life and talked about death and dying. When I asked what kinds of events they invited their mother to, the first responses were a bar mitzvah confirmation ceremony for a grandson, and a funeral. I said that I thought these sorts of events were likely to evoke depressive thoughts in Mrs. R, as were any other sorts of rituals or ceremonies no matter how objectively "joyous" they might appear to others.

I told Mrs. R and her children, as I had before, that Mrs. R was in a cycle of depression that would need considerable force to interrupt. I said that while she loved them and they loved her, they really didn't like each other very much, had often felt rejected by the other. I thought Mrs. R's mother's and her husband's deaths were important triggering incidents to destabilize the values that had characterized her life and that she had been unable to restore those values to their past stable configuration. Her most important resource at present was her therapist, who could provide antidepressant medication, reassurance, and some direction. I asked her individual therapist, who was present at the family interview, to continue to explore with Mrs. R what activities in the community might interest her that would require her to leave her apartment for some time each day, be part of a group, and engage in tasks she might enjoy. I asked her children not to give up inviting their mother to family affairs, and not to ask her to prepare these affairs herself under the impression that this would keep her busy. I asked them to keep in touch with her regularly by phone or visits, to make these visits brief, and to try not to feel too bad if she did not seem responsive. Finally, I offered to be available to Mrs. R and her family for interviews as needed. At the end of the meeting, I was able to obtain from all parties an expression of willingness to comply.

Postscript on Mrs. R

Approximately five months after Mrs. R left the hospital, along with her individual therapist I saw her and two of her children—the oldest, a son, and the next to youngest, a daughter—in the fourth family interview. Both children seemed pleased with their mother's progress out of hospital. They said she was doing well and was active: "We feel good because she feels good." They reported that she hosted a party for her grandchildren and all had a good time. Mrs. R resumed her volunteer work at a local hospital, and rejoined her circle of friends (e.g., she participated in a weekly bridge-playing group).

Her son, who in a previous interview had been outright hostile to me, was smiles and compliments on this occasion. He stated definitely that he had never seen his mother in a better mental condition, and attributed the remarkable change to a single comment I made at the previous meeting, that it would be relatively easy for Mrs. R to give up and spend the rest of her days in the hospital, but that was going to prove an awfully expensive "vacation." Her son interpreted his mother's response that she would be damned if she would give in to her depression, because that just wasn't the way to use the money her husband had left her. He complimented me for having told his mother the "truth" so bluntly, and his mother for her common sense and willpower.

My impression in this interview was that Mrs. R was holding her own, and that prospects were good that she would be able to fend off the "down" moods that she would probably experience from time to time, provided the human support system she now enjoyed continued at its current level of cohesion, and provided there was an absence of further sharp loss experiences. In terms of value diffusion theory, a favorable rebalancing of "continuity" and "discontinuity" values had occurred, effected to some extent by medication, a favorable nurturant experience while in the hospital, and a favorable posthospital experience with family members and friends negotiated by a significant contact in brief family therapy and brief individual therapy.

Discussion

The case of Mrs. R is not presented as a demonstration of a dramatically successful outcome of treatment, but rather to illustrate certain aspects of value diffusion theory. In the language of a psychodynamic theorist such as Abraham or Fenichel, Mrs. R's would probably be described as more an anaclitic depression than an introjective depression. In the language of the more recent psychodynamic theory of Arieti and Bemporad, Mrs. R demonstrated a Dominant Other rather than a Dominant Goal predisposition to depression. According to the cognitive viewpoint of Beck, Mrs. R's depression would be predicated on a socially dependent personality in contrast to an autonomous type. In Seligman's learned helplessness theory, her depression would stem from an induction into the role of a failure.

Value diffusion theory would agree with psychodynamic theory that Mrs. R's depression more resembled an anaclitic depression than an introjective depression, and more a Dominant Other and social dependent personality than a Dominant Goal and autonomous type of personality. But value diffusion theory would suggest only that the loss of her mother and later her husband served to trigger a destabilization of the configuration of "continuity" and "discontinuity" values that characterized her as a personality. Value diffusion theory does not posit that a loss in adulthood triggers the trauma of a loss experienced in infancy or early childhood, as does psychodynamic theory. Nursing her mother, Mrs. R expressed "continuity" values in a way that perhaps she could not express to her children or even her husband. When her mother died, these values were disrupted and there was an apparent failure of resources to restore them to their previous state. Nursing her husband, surely a prime representative of "discontinuity" values, she again was able to express "continuity" values. When his death occurred, there was another severe disruption of these values.

For the depressed person, the damage to "continuity" values is especially critical even in the case of a perceived failure to achieve a desired goal, which is essentially a "discontinuity" value. I would quibble some, therefore, with Beck's claim that depressed autonomous persons should necessarily be treated differently from depressed dependent persons. Both are in need of the restoration of disrupted "continuity" values, although he may well be correct about a somewhat different emphasis in treatment, inasmuch as problem solving for the depressed autonomous patient could have the same effect—restoration of "continuity" values—as support and reassurance for the depressed dependent patient.

I don't think that learned helplessness theory is very persuasive to explain Mrs. R's depressions. Of course when she was depressed, Mrs. R would complain that she was helpless; but this was not the case when she was not depressed and did not seem to be the case prior to the onset of her depressions. Dependency and helplessness can sometimes be confused, but from a psychological point of view it is essential to recognize the difference in the two states.

While value diffusion theory does not discard the central role of loss as a trigger for depression, it would hold that loss is not always necessary to produce depression. For instance, it would explain *postpartum* depression as not due to a loss but rather a destabilization of values produced by the birth of an infant, which has changed the status of a female from that of a *wife* (or mate) to that of a *mother*. What has occurred is not a loss but rather a change or shift from one prescribed role to another.

Klerman (1980) comments on the endogenous-reactive depression controversy, and notes that even in many so-called reactive depressions the nature of the life stress or experience of loss is not clear. Since value diffusion theory would redefine what constitutes life stress (as in the case of postpartum depression cited above) and does not require loss to precipitate depression, it might contribute to a reformulation of the old controversy that, despite its being downplayed in recent psychiatric diagnosis, still persists.

In my view, treatment of the depressive essentially requires the restoration of "continuity" values that have been severely disrupted. At the same time the restoration of "discontinuity" values is not inconsistent with the above statement, as the relative success of behavioral or cognitive therapies has demonstrated, since these therapies stress "discontinuity" values. Restoring "discontinuity" values can have the effect also of restoring "continuity" values in a depressed person.

Mrs. R did nicely in the hospital; there she recovered her normal mental status quickly. The hospital provided a secure, nurturant milieu ("continuity" values) in which she interacted with other individuals who were suffering more or less as she was, and who were usually sympathetic to each other's expressions of suffering (also "continuity" values). But outside the hospital, it was a different story. There she returned to her isolation—the thought of everyday routine, duties, regular work activities, keeping to a schedule, and taking initiative ("discontinuity" values) depleted her energy and she again became preoccupied by feelings of worthlessness that led to other signs of depression.

Outside the hospital, her individual therapist (who prescribed antidepressants and saw her in brief supportive psychotherapy) and her family (even though the relationship was strained and distant) served as important resources. The family interviews I conducted served as another source, and in these I encouraged her therapist and family to conduct a serious, sympathetic search to discover new activities in which Mrs. R would agree to participate to expand her resource network. Recently Greenblatt, Becerra, and Serafetinides (1982) described the importance of enrichment of the resource network for psychiatric patients, and made useful suggestions for how this might be carried out. In the state of Georgia there is a federally funded program in which older persons volunteer to spend a certain amount of time weekly with institutionalized children and adults, providing companionship and planning activities, and I suggested to Mrs. R's therapist that this program be explored for her.

While not strictly an advocate of brief psychotherapies, I believe they can be useful in treatment of depression because they are consistent with value diffusion theory. This view would hold for the psychoanalytically oriented brief therapies (e.g., as described by Sifneos, 1980) as well as for Beck's cognitive therapy and other behavioral therapies of depression (e.g., Lewinsohn's, 1974). It would hold for the systems oriented, brief marital and family therapies (e.g., those described by Zuk, 1975, 1981a; and by Stuart, 1980). In these brief therapies, however, it is essential that the therapist develop and maintain a relationship of trust with the depressed patient that can be counted upon presently and at times of future crisis, and not simply attend to the practical solving of presenting problems.

CHAPTER 6

ON THE PATHOLOGY OF BLAMING

A definition of family therapy is that it consists of means systematically applied to reduce pathogenic relating, which refers to (1) more or less conscious, assertive acts designed to obtain compliance and to punish failure to comply on the part of family or community, and (2) a style of relating or emotional climate in a family or community experienced as punitive despite apparent absence of punitive motives by those who appear responsible.

My experience in family therapy suggests that there are three forms of pathogenic relating most commonly observed: (1) silencing, (2) a style of relating or emotional climate which systematically sacrifices certain values at the expense of others, and (3) blaming. Of these three most common forms, blaming appears the commonest in interviews with families. All tend to produce loss of self-esteem in the victim, anxiety, anger, the feeling of being selected for punishment, and a motive of revenge or retaliation.

Previous papers have examined silencing (Zuk, 1965), and the pernicious effects of a style of relating which tends to produce victims who seek retaliation (Zuk, 1981b). In this paper I wish to examine blaming as a distinct, common form of pathogenic relating not previously discussed. It is utilized in some families far more than in others, but there is no family of my acquaintance that does not utilize it to some extent.

One intention of blaming is to produce shame, and it might be worthwhile to define both. Blaming refers to holding someone responsible for an act and blameful for it, hoping the victim will accept the judgment, be repentant and show shame. Shame refers to how the victim is supposed to feel and act. Not only is the victim supposed to feel "bad," but he or she is supposed to be repentant—that is, to undertake acts designed to bring an end to the blaming. These may be simple acts, as when one may appear humbled, or they may be complex, or they may be so ambiguous that the victim simply cannot know how to demonstrate the shame necessary to bring the blaming to a halt.

Pathogenic relating (Zuk, 1976) has its origins in a conflict of values, and two specific sets of values are frequently involved: the "continuity" set and the "discontinuity" set. Ordinarily these two sets of values are so mixed or intertwined in everyday relationships that it is hard to discern them. It is only when conflict reaches a certain intensity that the values begin to polarize, and they are more discernible as two distinct sets of values. The potential for pathogenic relating rises at this point, and one may see attempts by various parties to punish one another, such as in the case of blaming. The one blamed may even be scapegoated, which is a particularly intense form of blaming, for the scapegoat is subject to possible assault both physically and psychologically.

There are three clear steps in the blaming process. Step 1 is the polarization of values. Step 2 is the eruption of pathogenic relating and the selection of blaming as the particular form to be exercised. Step 3 consists of behavioral or psychiatric disturbances arising from blaming.

The Polarization of Values

An argument between husband and wife over who puts out the garbage may be quite harmless until one or the other comes to believe that more is at stake; that the issue is not simply who performs a household chore, but rather is one of fair play, or of manhood or womanhood. A person may feel that his or her identity is at stake, that the issue is so vital that the utmost effort to resist is required.

I have described the "continuity" and "discontinuity" value sets, and certain dysfunctions that result when these value sets become polarized due to intense, long-standing conflict. In a family it may happen, as I have suggested (Zuk, 1981b), that one set of values is systematically emphasized at the expense of the other. A case was described in which parents emphasized "discontinuity" values over "continuity" values, and it was surmised that the effect on the children was severe and disorienting. The children reacted antagonistically and each exhibited at a different point in their development symptoms of a psychiatric illness.

In another paper (Zuk, 1982) I analyzed the central characters in the film entitled *Ordinary People* for the presence of polarized values. In this movie, the mother—in a reversal of the more typical role in marriage—is the custodian of "discontinuity" values which she applies harshly in the case of a teenage son who survived an accident in which his favored brother dies. The mother is unable to nurture her surviving son; he feels blamed by her and guilty that his brother died instead of him. The son attempts suicide, but is spared from an untimely death by the interventions of other persons who are able to provide nurturance—a psychiatrist, his father, and a girl from school who takes an interest in him.

In a quite recent study (Zuk, 1983) I speculated on causes of a severe depression in an older woman, socially prominent in the Jewish community of a Deep-South town. Her beloved husband and mother had died after she had tended them lovingly. Her husband was a self-made wealthy man, but none of her children had his drive and ambition. She retreated from her children and friends, and from social obligations. She became deeply depressed and was hospitalized. I speculated that her depression was due to a "value diffusion," which signifies a kind of personality disorganization. Her role in life depended so heavily on the presence of her husband and, to an extent, her mother, that when they died it disintegrated. According to the psychoanalytic theory depression is attributed to two types of losses: (1) a loss of relationships, and (2) a loss of achievements. The woman had suffered a loss of the first type—of relationships. It seemed to me of interest that the losses posited by psychoanalytic theory fit within the value systems that I have posited and that seem to underlie so much of family life: the loss of relationships is a loss in "continuity" values; and the loss of achievements is a loss of "discontinuity" values.

The Selection of Blaming as Pathogenic Relating

Blaming derives from the universal human interest in determining the cause of events—even when the cause cannot be known or when an inaccurate determination is made. This is especially true for surprising or shocking events in which injury occurs. To assess cause in these events is tantamount to assessing blame.

For example, *The New York Times* stated in headlines that a commission investigating the deaths by terrorist bombing of 241 United States marines in Lebanon "blames" their commanders for failing to take adequate precautions. Probably the commission report itself does not use the word "blame," but it is used in the newspaper headline. What is implied in the commission report is made explicit in the newspaper account, in part because of the newspaper's "mission" to dramatize events for the benefit of its readers.

President Reagan's declared assumption of personal responsibility for the Lebanon tragedy seemed for the moment to take the wind out of the sails of those, both inside and outside the military, hoping for someone on whom to pin the blame, a scapegoat. The trauma of the event for the American public, plus the limited capacity to strike back at the actual perpetrators, seemed to have intensified the hunt for a scapegoat at home. The President himself was not an acceptable scapegoat because he was too far removed from the immediate chain of command.

Blaming tends to be a rather aggressive act, and there can be little question that it originates in anger and produces anger in the victim, but to the extent that it manages to produce shame in the victim, he or she is constrained from retaliating. For instance, mother blames little Johnny for tearing up a photo of grandma and grandpa. Johnny hears his mother call him a bad little boy. He is upset to see the way mother looks at him. She insists that he say he is sorry. Now Johnny may still wonder what he has done wrong, but he cannot mistake mother's upset. This distracts him from his anger at being caught by mother, he gulps hard, and says the words mother wants to hear.

"Don't Blame Me; It's Your Fault!"

At 7 or 8 years of age parents begin to hear the plaintive cry from their children, "Don't blame me; it's your fault!" It is an interesting phrase to examine in children, for it is frequently used in situations where it does not seem to apply. For instance, a child forgets to put her coat on in the morning, is reminded to by her mother, and replies, "Don't blame me; it's your fault!" The mother may be quite dumbstruck.

Mother will continue to be puzzled so long as she takes the child's comment literally, rather than as an attempt by the daughter to exert some control in the relationship. Children are so often the object of reminders to do one thing or the other by parents, that it becomes a matter of some import to seek to stem the flow of such reminders. Through such reminders, and by other means, children learn about being blamed. They learn that the reminders make them feel uneasy, as if they have done something wrong or bad. A reasonably alert child will try to see if the process "works the other way too"; that is, whether he or she can make mommy or daddy feel uneasy (bad) by reminders. What it is not so easy for the child to control is the appropriateness or rationality of the process; that is, there is a tendency for the child to generalize words or phrases too much in the service of controlling relationships and situations. The child hopes that "Don't blame me; it's your fault!" will shut a parent up, will bring an end to a demand or reminder, even though it "makes no sense" in a particular context.

Illustration

A few months before this was written, I called to my daughter, who is 8 years old, to come and get Diggety, our rambunctious 2-year-old mixed-breed dog which was running loose in a fenced-in area. I knew Diggety would respond better to my daughter than to me, and so I called for Gaby. While opening the gate, Gaby let the dog get by her and run off. I was a bit sarcastic to my daughter, who pursued the dog but soon gave up and went back into the house. There she told her mother what had happened. I was finally able to retrieve the animal myself, and went into the house. I saw that Gaby was still upset, and told her I knew it wasn't her fault. Thereupon she blurted out—not at me but at her mother—"It's your fault!"

Now, I cannot be certain why my daughter chose her mother rather than me as the object of her wrath, but so she did. It is possible that at her age, Gaby has some special task to complete in her relationship with her mother as compared with me, or that the task is one that must be accomplished earlier. Whatever the "psychological" reason for the remark, there was no mistaking it.

Erik Erikson (1950) has suggested that if everything goes back to childhood, then everything is somebody else's fault. What Erikson seems to mean is that the person who finds fault with everything and everyone is neurotic, because that is a characteristic of the child. Alfred Adler (1956) agrees that the life plan of the neurotic demands that if he fails it should be through someone else's fault. Erikson and Adler remind us of the importance of blaming, that it is "normal" for the child, but that if it remains a cornerstone of the adult personality, then that person has a neurotic disposition.

Illustration

> A sister exhibited a lifelong jealousy of her brother, whom she felt was favored by her mother. Following her mother's death, there was a dispute over the estate because the brother was suspicious of the role played by the sister's husband, a lawyer who prepared the mother's will. The brother brought suit against the brother-in-law, charging him with removing money that legally belonged to the estate. The court ordered the money returned. At the trial the sister had an uncle and aunts testify on behalf of her husband.
>
> Immediately following the trial, the sister told her uncle and aunts that she would have nothing more to do with them, as they had humiliated her husband. The relatives were astounded by her attitude; still, they felt guilty that they had indeed injured their niece in some unclear way. Their niece maintained her attitude against them for years.

My interpretation of what happened in this case is as follows: (1) the sister exhibited the neurotic's lifelong skill at blaming others; and (2) by making her relatives feel guilty, she managed subtly to protect her husband from further retaliation by her brother, as her brother might conclude that "enough is enough" and that further punishment of his sister and brother-in-law would be unwarranted and excessive.

Emotional Disorders Related to Blaming

Harry Stack Sullivan (1953) proposed the term "paranoid transformation" for the pathological process by which blame is passed from one person to others. Regarding the dynamics of the paranoid transformation, he said,

In these situations, it is now impossible to maintain reasonable dissociation of previously dissociated tendencies in one's personality which are still, in terms of the personified self, *apart*. As a result, that which was dissociated, and which was in a certain meaningful sense related to the not-me, is definitely *personified* as not-me—that is, as others. And the others carry the blame for that which had previously had to be maintained in dissociation as an intolerable aspect of one's own personal possibilities.

Now, at the beginning of this transformation the only impression one has is of a person in the grip of horror, of uncanny devastation which makes everything threatening beyond belief. But if the person is not utterly crushed by the process, he can begin rather rapidly to elaborate personifications of evil creatures. And in this process of personifying the specific evil, the transformation begins to move fast, since it's wonderfully successful in one respect: it begins to put on these others—people who are outside him, his enemies—everything which he has clearly formulated in himself as defect, blamable weakness, and so on. . . . Under these circumstances, needless to say, he arrives at a state which is pretty hard to remedy—by categorical name, a paranoid state. (pp. 361–362)

For Sullivan the paranoid transformation was an intrapsychic process more likely to occur in persons with low self-esteem than in others. Once activated, of course, it transformed the interpersonal world of the person; it was the process that formed the bona fide bigot, the bona fide paranoid.

Sullivan must have been aware of the "natural history" of blaming which, in certain individuals with a fragile self, promoted the paranoid transformation; but, to the best of this writer's knowledge, he did not elaborate on that natural history. The claim of this paper is that there is a natural history of the blaming process, and that for certain individuals there are disabling consequences. It must also be stressed that blaming is "normal" in human relationships—for one reason, because it is so common; for another, because it is just one step away from that most human of enterprises, the search for causes of events.

It is even conceivable that "learning about blaming" is an important acquisition in children and adolescents, and is an essential prerequisite for the acquisition of a normal capacity for guilt in adolescence and young adulthood. Psychoanalysis, which has placed such a heavy burden on guilt as a contributing cause of neurosis, has also advanced the idea that it is an important cornerstone of civilization. Guilt can become perverted in numerous ways, but it is also essential to the maintenance of the sense of obligation that humans have toward one another, and to the urge to correct obligations that have been violated.

Two clinical cases will be presented in which the blaming process is apparent, and in which the outcomes of that process seem more dysfunctional or destructive than functional or constructive.

Case 1

A bright, 16-year-old boy was placed in a residential treatment setting because of drug abuse and other delinquencies. His parents found it hard to
handle him, and there was an occasional fistfight between his father and
him. His mother tried to act as intermediary, without much success. He did
rather well in the residential setting, where he received various therapies,
including family therapy, and he was returned home after a few months.
For several weeks he appeared stable and cooperative: he obtained part-
time employment, bought an automobile with money he earned, and applied to a local college and was accepted. But after about 6 weeks, there
were signs of a serious deterioration: he was reported to be using drugs
again, was associating with drug-using youngsters, and was writing bank
checks for which he had no funds.

One day the family therapists were called frantically by the parents. The
boy was perched in a tree about 40 feet above ground in their backyard,
and was threatening to jump. After several hours he was persuaded to
come down, was taken into police custody, and was returned to the residential setting at which he had been placed. For about two weeks he remained in a very hostile state, needed to be restrained, and was given
psychotropic medications to calm him down.

After four or five weeks another discharge was being discussed for the
boy because of the substantial improvement in behavior he showed. The
discharge was effected, but this time the boy did not return to his parents'
home; rather, he was accepted into the home of an older friend. This ar-
rangement had the approval of the parents.

The reason for reporting this case is the presence of intense blaming between the boy, his mother, and stepfather, with serious consequences for his
behavior and theirs. The boy never forgave his mother for her remarriage; the
stepfather could not forgive the boy for an intensely rebellious attitude toward
him. The mother was caught in the middle, trying desperately to placate two
parties who were unwilling to compromise.

The boy and his stepfather were in a chronic state of rage against each other.
For the stepfather, the son represented the degradation of "continuity" values:
he obeyed no rules, hated authority, and wouldn't "listen to reason." For the
son, the stepfather represented the degradation of "discontinuity" values: he
was harsh, authoritarian, unemotional. They held each other to be at fault; neither would give an inch. The result was that both were driven to extreme be-
haviors. The extreme behavior of the younger was sufficient to have him placed
in a residential treatment setting for the emotionally disturbed. The extreme behavior of the older was sufficient to jeopardize his marriage, and made it difficult for him to function well at work.

Case 2

A black couple had gone to great trouble to have a 12-year-old adopted son placed in a residential treatment center. All the children in this family of bright, well-educated parents had been adopted; the hospitalized child was the oldest of them and also the most recently adopted. The other children had been adopted in infancy or early childhood, but the "disturbed" child was not adopted until about age 8.

The family had recently moved from a town in the Northeast United States to a smaller town in the Deep South, where they experienced some culture shock. The father said that he never felt his race as much as he did in the town, even though he was affiliated with a college and enjoyed a certain status in the college. The trouble with the son started before the family's move to the South. It was reported that he lied, stole money from his parents and children at school, and entered neighbors' houses without being asked.

The admitting psychiatric diagnosis was conduct disorder, but shortly afterward this diagnosis was withdrawn and a diagnosis emphasizing a disturbance in parent-child relations was reached and maintained until his discharge. Although the boy did not perform well on intelligence tests, it was felt he was bright and he was certainly an articulate, alert youngster.

This was a child who had been moved about from foster parent to foster parent. He resented his adoptive parents' attitude toward him, and they had come to bitterly resent him. He had told them that if he were white, and they were white, there would be no problem because nothing would be made of his behavior. Of course this assertion enraged these parents who stated in a family interview that they couldn't tolerate a bigot in their home.

An effort to engage the family in therapy proved fruitless. The parents resented the notion that in any way they were associated with the problems of the boy. The therapists were told that if they reviewed the records properly, they could reach no other conclusion but that the boy had a mental illness. When the therapists countered that, whatever the findings might be psychiatrically with respect to the boy, it would be helpful to have their cooperation in a treatment program, the parents angrily rejected the position. After several sessions with the parents, it seemed clear that their position was that the boy should remain hospitalized indefinitely, and that treatment should focus on correcting a defect in the boy that was causing his deviant behavior.

The boy's behavior in the hospital showed lack of support for a psychiatric diagnosis, and this was conveyed to the parents, who bitterly rejected the professional opinion. (They implied that the therapists were not very competent.) The therapists then made two points clearly to the parents. One was that in the apparent absence of a psychiatric illness, it was necessary for the boy to be removed from the hospital and returned home; that the parents could try to find a suitable school placement for him, and seek outpatient psychiatric treatment if an agency agreed with the premise that he needed such treatment. The second point was that if the parents found that they could not manage the boy themselves, an alternative was to place him with another family through an appropriate social welfare agency.

The communication of the two-point plan was greeted by a storm of protest. Now it was entirely clear to the parents how incompetent the therapists were, and how ineffective the hospital placement was. The reply to the parents was that if they really believed such things, they should remove their son immediately. Paradoxically, the parents did not want their son removed! They said the therapists and hospital were now under an obligation to keep the child because they failed to make the proper diagnosis.

Despite the parents' protestations, accusations (and recommendations), the child was promptly discharged to the parents, according to the plan of the therapists.

The therapists believed that their appraisal of the boy and his parents was correct. Family therapy was recommended, but the parents refused to cooperate. What they really wanted was to unburden themselves of this boy, who was being scapegoated. Here was a child who did not conform to their idealized notion of themselves as parents, and it was intolerable. At the same time they could not admit, to themselves and to others, that they wanted to get rid of this boy because to admit that would mean that they had failed to live up to that idealized notion.

I do not think it is going too far to say that the boy was a victim of a paranoid transformation operating particularly in his father, but with the cooperation of his mother. I visualize that the boy was the object of the father's negative projection on whites and white society. Because the therapists appeared in the father's eyes allied with the son (and were white), they were also recipients of his paranoid transformation. Once, even, he alluded to the therapists' WASP mentality (although both are white, neither is a WASP). If it is not already clear, I believe that the *father* suffered from a paranoia focused on his son. To be sure, it was a well-contained paranoia. In ordinary conversation, he was rational, alert, "appropriate." But on the subject of his son, he was psychotic.

The reader who likes to play devil's advocate might respond to my position as follows: "Maybe the parents were right; that is, maybe the boy had a genuine conduct disorder, in which case he would have had a psychiatric illness. Just because the parents didn't agree with the therapists' judgment regarding diagnosis, that doesn't make them paranoid." My response would be as follows: the diagnosis was probably correct; but no one can be 100 percent sure about a diagnosis. Whether the diagnosis was 100 percent correct or not, my case against the parents is built·on their extraordinary reaction. They denounced the therapists and the hospital, but refused to accept the removal of the son from the control of the therapists and hospital. According to them, the son was a bigot because he thought there were instances in which blacks and whites were treated differently, and he lived in a society which favored whites over blacks. According to them, the son must have a mental illness because they knew that he had taken money from them and had lied to them. I suggest to the devil's advocate that the case they built against their son was excessive, and that the *character* of the case was psychotic in the sense that it was essentially irrational and hateful.

My devil's advocate might reply, "Well, what you have here is an instance of black parents who are oversensitive on the question of race. Racism exists; it is not paranoia. You are confusing psychopathology with the historic injustice suffered by blacks in a white-dominated society. The boy does sound like a bigot." My reply would be as follows: I have heard *blacks* refer to each other in fairly derogatory terms, but they are not called bigots. What is this child saying that deserves the term "bigot"? I don't follow you. He is calling attention to the fact that in this society whites and blacks are often treated differently, and that whites seem the most favored. Is that bigotry, or is it simply a reasonably accurate assessment of race relations in the United States even in the 1980s? Now, on the question of racism—white or black—and psychopathology: is the true bigot mentally ill? I would have to say yes because it seems to me that the true bigot has a true paranoia; at the same time, I would have to warn that most of those who are called bigots—whites or blacks—are not true bigots and do not fit the definition for a psychopathology. I want to stress that it was a gross misperception on the part of the father to call his son a bigot. The only way he could have done that, in my estimation, is if he had completely lost control of his racially based rage, and had settled on his son as the safest depository of that rage. That was paranoid; that was psychotic.

The Lethality of Blaming

A good example of the lethality that may be an outcome of the blaming process is the altercation that may occur between two automobile drivers that may result in the serious injury or death of one or both. I am not talking about the auto accident, but the case where one driver or the other believes his "rights" have been violated, and believes there is a need to prove it to the other.

Police officials are aware that this is not an infrequent occurrence and that a significant number of injuries and deaths are the result each year in the United States. For instance, in 1983 in newspapers in the state of Texas several homicides were reported in which drivers had apparently violated the "norm" of using the automobile horn very sparingly. Out-of-state drivers were not aware of this "norm," and tended to be the victims of the assaults, which in several instances resulted in their death.

It may be remembered that during the Arab oil embargo in 1974 in the United States, numerous instances of physical assault and some deaths were reported in cases where drivers tried to move past others waiting in line at a gasoline pump, or when drivers were told by attendants that they could not fill their gas tanks.

It is rather odd that normally quite sane, controlled, rational individuals will react with atypical rage when they believe their driving "rights" have been violated, and from a purely objective point of view these violations may appear quite trivial. But despite the apparent triviality, the most serious consequences may follow.

Not the gun but the automobile is the "great equalizer" in modern society. It breaks barriers of social class, race, religion. It is obviously a machine of great power—of great destructive power—that is crucial to the maintenance of society. The United States is, figuratively if not literally, a "society on wheels." The blaming process, as expressed on the city streets, roads, and highways of America by persons operating automobiles, motorcycles and trucks, is unique, different than that expressed in homes, offices, shops, plants, or even airplanes or ships.

A final comment on the blaming process as expressed while occupying an automobile may be in order: it has to do with the oath probably repeated thousands of times daily on America's highways, "Woman driver!" From a psychological point of view, it is an interesting phrase. Almost always it is made by a man and directed against a driver identified as a female who has violated a rule recognized by the man as valid. The woman is blamed as an offender of the rule, *but she is not blamed as an individual but as a class.* "Woman driver!" is one of those almost-institutionalized forms of male chauvinism. The capacities of women to think rationally, operate equipment safely, negotiate complex tasks competently, are derogated. Their capacity to function well in a world dominated by "discontinuity" values is minimized by men.

CHAPTER 7

THE TRUNCATED NUCLEAR FAMILY

Truncated nuclear family is the term I have used since the late '70s for the family in which husband and wife live together but are estranged, and where the children side with their mothers against their fathers. Physical separation or divorce is a common outcome, as well as behavioral and psychiatric disorders in family members. As I see it, the truncated nuclear family is the garden-variety family psychopathology in the United States today.

In therapy the family usually presents a variety of complaints. One of the commonest is "difficulty communicating," a catchy phrase that usually means the members know perfectly well what the others want, but aren't prepared to give it. Many families come with a member who presents a rather specific problem: the adolescent abusing drugs, the mother who is depressed, the father who drinks too much, the young adult who has experienced a first psychotic episode.

Family therapy typically signifies that the nuclear family (two generations, spouses and their children) is seen for interviews once weekly for four to six months. The interview schedule may vary somewhat, and the length of time the family is seen may vary somewhat, but most family therapy is typically once weekly for four to six months. That is not because therapists prefer it that way, but because *families* do. Families do not particularly like being scrutinized by experts, but will submit to it for a while if there is a pressing need. It's a bit like going to the dentist only when the tooth really hurts. (Unfortunately, some family therapists talk and write as if families love the experience.)

I have been seeing families in therapy for 25 years, which is about as long as the field has existed. The basic theory is that disturbed family relationships are an important causative factor in mental illness, which is not so remarkable a viewpoint because it has been accepted for a long time that good family relationships are conducive to the development of healthy personalities.

I have treated a wide range of behavioral, psychiatric, or "relationship" problems in families from many origins. For most of my professional life, I worked in Philadelphia, a metropolitan Northeastern city in the United States composed of distinct ethnic neighborhoods. There are the South Philadelphia Italians, the Blacks and Puerto Ricans of North Philadelphia, the Jews and Irish of Northeast Philadelphia, and the Main Line Philadelphia WASPS. One learns to be sensitive to the different family traditions. Some allow outsiders more access than others, although all will limit access at some point. The good therapist understands the limits families impose, and tries not to push beyond them.

The therapist hears a hodgepodge of family conflict, and the problem is to bring order out of chaos. I discovered in the middle 70s that most family conflict was *value* conflict, and typically that two sets of values were involved. These I came to call the "continuity" and the "discontinuity." Oddly enough, in the family that was functioning reasonably well, it was often difficult to discern these antithetical values; they presented themselves most clearly in conflict. Conflict revealed a set of *continuity* values that emphasized emotional closeness, the wholeness or unity of relationships, nurturance and caretaking, and the superiority of intuition over rationality. Conflict also revealed a set of *discontinuity* values that emphasized rationality, personal achievement, law and order, codes of conduct, and systematic procedure. (Please note that these are not the dictionary definitions for continuity and discontinuity.)

The reason conflict reveals these distinct value sets underlying family relationships is that conflict by definition is a condition in which ideas, attitudes, and beliefs tend to be polarized. In conflict persons tend to express their ideas, attitudes, and beliefs *forcefully*; there is a greater tendency for differences to be emphasized. When the family is functioning "normally," differences tend to be minimized, relatively absent, muted, or quickly resolved.

Husband-wife conflict can involve literally hundreds of issues over which there are serious differences, but at bottom one perceives common elements in the way these differences are expressed: wife accuses husband of being uninvolved, unemotional and distant, too judgmental, too much a disciplinarian (especially where the children are involved), and overly rational; whereas husband accuses wife of being over-emotional, disorganized, laissez faire (especially where the children are concerned), and too heavily reliant on intuition to guide conduct. Essentially, husband blames wife for holding continuity values, whereas wife blames husband for his discontinuity values.

But one also finds continuity-discontinuity values polarized in conflict between parents and children. The parents claim the children are disobedient, untrustworthy, break agreements. The children claim the parents are authoritarian, too harsh in discipline, unmindful that other children are treated more humanely. Here the parents blame their children for the continuity values, and the children blame the parents for the discontinuity values.

And, finally, one finds continuity-discontinuity values polarized in family-community conflict. The family claims the community (embodied in the neighborhood) is too rule- and regulation-conscious, whereas the community claims the family wants special privileges. At another level or dimension, this is also an enactment of conflicted continuity and discontinuity values.

The *predictability* with which the various parties (husband-wife, parent-child, and family-community) espouse one set of values or the other is striking. Although there are numerous exceptions to the rule, the rule is that in husband-wife conflict, husbands will espouse discontinuity values; in parent-child conflict, parents will espouse discontinuity values; and in family-community conflict, the community will espouse discontinuity values.

It is of some historic interest that the exponents of continuity values (wives, children, and family) have been in a somewhat weaker position than those (husbands, parents, and community) that have been main exponents of discontinuity values—weaker in the physical, or economic or political sense; but this should not be taken to mean that power alone determines the values parties espouse. While it is a fact that males are physically stronger than females, and that parents and the community have historically exercised greater economic and political power than children or wives, it is not uncommon for husbands or parents to report that they feel helpless toward their wives or children, or for the community to feel that it cannot influence or control the family. In other words, physical or economic power alone does not explain why the parties espouse the values they do; other factors (biology, life cycle, cultural) must play major causative roles. Also, circumstances may change allegiances. For example, in a parent-child conflict wives will frequently join their husbands against children; and in a husband-wife conflict, the community will frequently side with the wife. Normally wives and children share continuity values, and husbands and community share discontinuity values, but there are exceptions to the rule.

Conflict that markedly polarizes values, and that persists over time, produces what I have referred to as pathogenic relating, which denotes ways of relating in families that are especially stressful and harmful, and increase the risk of members becoming symptomatic and even severely mentally disturbed. The three major forms of pathogenic relating that I have observed are, (1) blaming, (2) silencing, and (3) "style of relating" in which certain values are systematically favored over others to produce a disturbed family structure. A lot of blaming and silencing occurs in families, and much of it is relatively harmless; it is when they are "driven" by values that have been profoundly polarized, that they are no longer harmless. Then blaming and silencing (family members shutting each other up) become quite destructive, quite disorganizing. A "style of relating" in families that consistently favors one set of values over another greatly increases the risk of pathogenic relating. In a case study for a professional journal in 1981, I speculated that the profound commitment of parents to discontinuity values was causally related to a psychiatric illness in each of their three children. The absence of continuity values (for instance, the scarcity of physical affection) created a resentment in the children that was profoundly disorganizing as they moved into adolescence. In their own way, these parents loved their children—but that love was not enough because it failed to provide the intimate physical nurturance that children seem to require for normal physical, mental, and emotional growth.

Although the process may have begun earlier, since World War II the US economy, particularly the emergence of the new technologies, has placed a premium on the relatively small nuclear family as compared with the less mobile traditional or extended family. From the end of World War II through the 1970s approximately 20 percent of Americans moved every year. (Only in the early '80s does the percentage seem to be dropping slightly.) The promise of employment or of improved job prospects moved families, and the nuclear family enjoyed a clear advantage in the job market. At the same time, it was recognized that the nuclear family was a more fragile unit than the traditional or extended family. Heavy demands were placed on parents to meet the social and emotional developmental needs of children—demands that at one time were shared with relatives. Now the relatives were simply not there.

The energies of the husband-father to share child-bearing responsibilities with his wife were drained by the demands of the workplace. He *provided*, but that did not necessarily mean that he *nurtured*. The brunt of the child-bearing task was left to the wife-mother, and resentment and bitterness toward the husband-father were common. Children, earlier attuned and more sensitive to the emotional state of their mothers than their fathers, recognized her resentment, her bitterness, and eventually identified the source as their fathers. They sided with their mothers against their fathers, and their siding was to have a dramatic effect on their capacity to learn and relate to others.

By siding with their mothers, children sided predominantly with their mothers' continuity values; by siding against their fathers, children sided against their fathers' predominantly discontinuity values. Thus it was insured that the children would be doubly antagonistic to discontinuity values such as personal achievement and discipline. The children would resent authority, and mothers could not neutralize this resentment because the continuity values they mainly represented to their children did not hold out authority as a positive value.

While there has been a premium on the more mobile nuclear family in the United States, especially since World War II, it is a vulnerable family unit because of its fragility, and the truncated nuclear family is a sign of its vulnerability. It is the typical way the nuclear family breaks down under stress. The emotional estrangement between the spouses often leads to actual physical separation or divorce. The poor school performance and disciplinary problems of the children are established by research, but narcissism and alienation are also characteristics of the children as they move through adolescence into young adulthood.

In a paper originally written in German in 1932, the psychologist Erich

Fromm speculated that Western societies were moving from what he called a patriarchal to a matriarchal structure. He cited J.J. Bachofen, the German philosopher-sociologist, who in 1861 published his book *Mother Right*. According to Bachofen, the matriarchal principle is that of life, unity, and peace. Through caring for her infant, the mother extends her love beyond herself to others with the aim of preserving and beautifying the existence of others. The matriarchal principle is that of universality, whereas the patriarchal principle is that of restriction. Fromm noted that certain matriarchal tendencies could be observed in radical youth, and suggested that a purely matriarchal society would stand in the way of full development of the individual because of motherly overindulgence and infantilization of the child. On the other hand, Fromm commented that the purely patriarchal society cares nothing for love and equality, and is concerned only with manmade laws, the state, abstract principles, and obedience.

The matriarchal principle that Bachofen and Fromm talked about is clearly within the framework of what I have referred to as continuity values; and the patriarchal principle, within the framework of discontinuity values. Fromm described character or personality deviations in individuals that would likely result when a *society* was too greatly biased in the direction of matriarchy or patriarchy. I have referred to similar deviations in individuals that are likely to result when a *family* is too greatly biased in the direction of either continuity or discontinuity values.

The exact number of truncated nuclear families in the United States is unknown, but divorce statistics (the yearly number of divorces passed the one million mark in the latter half of the 1970s) suggest that the number in any one year must be in the several millions. The single-parent family (headed in 9 out of 10 cases by a mother) has had a remarkable increase in the past decade. The US Census Bureau calculated that in 1981 there were over eight million families composed of a fatherless home managed by a woman with children aged from birth through 17 years. If present trends continue, a child born in 1983 will have a 40 percent chance of seeing his or her parents divorce, and a 20 percent chance of experiencing a second parental divorce. While not synonymous with the truncated nuclear family, the single-parent family was probably a truncated nuclear family at one time in its history.

Where would one look if one wanted to locate the truncated nuclear family in density today? The answer is, the Silicon Valley. This is an area in Northern California (south of San Francisco) that has become perhaps the most prominent high-technology center in the United States. This area has been portrayed as a vision of postindustrial society in which fortunes can be made overnight in electronics and computers. But reports are emerging that all is not well in the Silicon Valley. The high-pressure environment is taking its toll in divorce, alcoholism, spouse and child abuse, and drug dependency. The divorce rate in Santa Clara County (in which the Silicon Valley is located) is 7.1 per thousand population, versus 5.8 for California as a whole, and 5.3 for the entire United States. Local authorities believe that child and drug abuse are much worse than in comparable metropolitan areas elsewhere.

The truncated nuclear family is depicted in recent motion pictures that have had a tremendous impact on audiences. *Kramer vs. Kramer* and *Ordinary People* (see Chapter 4) are two such films. *Kramer vs. Kramer* is about a relatively recent significant phenomenon in American family life: the educated middle-class young wife who is dissatisfied and leaves her husband and young son for a career. She chooses discontinuity over continuity values, which requires her husband to decide how much he can provide his son of continuity values (nurturing, caretaking) lost through the wife's departure.

Ordinary People is a superb film in which a variation of the truncated nuclear family is portrayed. The wife-mother (well-educated, upper middle-class, white, probably Protestant) is the major exponent in the family of *discontinuity* values. Her favored teenage son has drowned in a boating accident which a somewhat younger son survived. The younger son is guilt-ridden. He makes a suicide attempt, survives, and is hospitalized. He returns home to find his mother unresponsive, still silently mourning the death of her beloved one. The husband-father is caught between his wife and son. Which one needs him more; to which is he more responsible? Ultimately he must make a choice, and it is the son. He provides the continuity values the son had hungered for.

In American television soap operas the truncated nuclear family is depicted ad nauseam. Part of the fascination of the public for such epics as *Dallas* and *Dynasty* is due, I think, to the intense value conflict portrayed, the eruption of pathogenic relating, the rising potential for or actual outbreak of violence, and then the temporary restoration of benign family functioning. The audience is taken through the full cycle of events in which a violent clash of values is needed to drive the cycle forward.

Family therapy can be a very important treatment for the truncated nuclear family. The therapist must be skilled in the diversity of family backgrounds, in order to be able to detect those elements which may affect the family's level of readiness for therapy. (Families differ greatly in their readiness to undertake the stress of therapy.) The therapist must be skilled in detecting the core of value conflict through the maze of conflict reported by family members. The therapist must be able to detect the forms of pathogenic relating that have erupted in the aftermath of value conflict. Then the therapist must skillfully enact the three main therapeutic roles available to him or her as the best means to intervene in pathogenic relating, to minimize or reduce it, thus to create a more favorable climate for the resolution of value conflict.

Rather homely names were given to two of the three roles that I think the family therapist is obliged to enact skillfully. One is that of go-between; the other is that of side-taker. The third role was given a somewhat more mellifluous title: celebrant.

As go-between, the therapist either facilitates communication among family members, or restricts or limits it. As side-taker, the therapist takes sides on issues discussed in family interviews, and may side with or against family members. As celebrant, the therapist is a significant *presence* at the time of a crisis in the family—a child who has run away, a suicide attempt, a husband's or wife's first depression or psychotic episode. The celebrant role has traditionally been assigned to the clergyman, physician, or lawyer, among other respected community authority figures, but recently the psychotherapist is also being invested with that mantle. Unlike the role of go-between or side-taker, the therapist cannot assume the celebrant role, but must be *invested* with it by the distressed family. The condition of crisis raises the chance that the family will look to the therapist as a celebrant, as one who can help restore sanity out of disorder.

By moving skillfully in family interviews from one therapeutic role to another, by skillfully enacting these roles, by skillful timing of these interventions, the therapist hopes to minimize or reduce pathogenic relating in the family so that a healing can take place of a rupture involving deeply held values. Each role is a coin with two faces. For instance, when as go-between the therapist attempts to facilitate communication among family members, he or she is essentially espousing a continuity value; but when he or she attempts to restrict or limit communication as go-between, that expresses a discontinuity value. When as celebrant the therapist suggests that family members forgive each other for transgressions, that is expressing a continuity value; but when he or she suggests sternly that justice must be done and discipline meted out, that is expressing a discontinuity value. Thus in enacting the three therapeutic roles, the therapist not only "attacks" pathogenic relating directly, but also its underlying cause, the polarization of values that has produced a dysfunctional family.

There are a number of types of family therapy today and most are based on a concept of pathogenic relating; most, also, are based on a concept of roles (like those of go-between, side-taker, and celebrant) enacted by the therapist as interventions to reduce pathogenic relating; and most are based on a concept that the dysfunctional family is one in which a profound *value* conflict has occurred among members.

In my judgment, family therapy is the psychotherapy of choice for the truncated nuclear family, but is not a panacea. Many families are unwilling to face the real or fantasied stress. Also, family therapy is a relatively new development, and the number of fully competent therapists is still relatively small—probably not more than a couple of thousand (although the number of mental health practitioners treating families today may approximate 40,000 in the United States). Steps are being taken by organizations such as the American Association for Marriage and Family Therapy, headquartered in Washington, D.C., to upgrade standards.

The truncated nuclear family is a price that Western societies have had to pay for their emphasis on the individual, on personal achievement. The benefit has been a burst of creativity affecting all spheres of human interest: art, science, technology, government, industry, social institutions. The cost is grounded in the biological, psychological, and sociological fact that change is stressful, and that humans have a varying but limited capacity to adapt to change.

PART II

DIAGNOSIS, TECHNIQUE, AND CHANGE

CHAPTER 1

CONVERSATION WITH RESIDENTS: PART I

The conversations reported here and in Chapter 2 of Part II were recorded on successive Wednesdays in late August, 1973. Present with me in the recording studio were several 2nd and 3rd year psychiatric residents from the Eastern Pennsylvania Psychiatric Institute, and one 3rd year resident from the Medical College of Pennsylvania. Their names are as follows: Drs. P. Cupple, M. Doria, S. McLeer, R. Palmieri, K. Park, and M. Shovelin. Not all were present at both recording sessions which were videotaped. Most were beginning to carry their first family therapy cases. I was providing at the time personal supervision of a case carried by one of the residents, Cupple, and the conversation of August 22nd, 1973, begins with his comments.

In preparing the transcripts it simplified matters and yet did not seem a violation of their rights, to signify the residents' comments by the letter R. My comments are designated by Z. In the conversation reported in Chapter 2 we are joined by one of my trainees who is not a resident, Reverend A. Bambrick, a priest, whose comments are designated by the letter T.

The conversations are wide-ranging, covering relatively narrow items on technique and diagnosis. But they also move to more universal issues, such as the relation of the individual to his family, and the viability of such concepts as family systems and family change.

The transcripts required editing to improve readability, and I exercised that editorial prerogative.

Discussion of August 22, 1973

R: (A resident is reviewing a case supervised by Dr. Zuk) If he wanted to he could go to Minnesota and work for one final year for the company and, well, do whatever he wanted to do. So they transferred him out and he decided to take the job because it paid so well. It was a very fine-paying job, and he had a good job before that with the company. So he went out to Minnesota, left his family here, and while out in Minnesota, after about three months at work, he developed this very strange neurological illness where he became very weak in the arms and legs and he lost a lot of weight. And he is still thinner than he used to

R: be, and he still can't use his arms as well as he should. He has this lack of motor power that he once had. He was in the hospital like six weeks out there, and finally after he was well enough they did send him home to his family and his job terminated.

Z: He left? This connects it better for me because I understood something slightly different. He was in the job with the company for 16 years here in Philadelphia. The job was being terminated here, and he was given the option of one year in the Middle West. He took that but that meant he would also have to leave his family for that period of time. Was he given also any clear assurance of his job there?

R: Not at all. He was rather well-assured that he wouldn't.

Z: But somehow he felt that he had to take that type of—Extremely difficult choice, wasn't it?

R: He's in his fifties and I think he felt he couldn't.

Z: He does not move to a job in an area where he spent so many years and where he raised his family. He takes a job which removes him from his family. This is only two or three years ago?

R: This is the very same year that our patient became ill in college. There's a very strong connection there.

Z: It is the same year she became—

R: Uhuh.

Z: Yeah, the symptoms you were describing sound similar between father and daughter.

R: At Christmas time she wrote him a very long letter because the mother—

Z: What kind; what did she write him?

R: The mother wrote to the daughter and said, your Dad hasn't heard from you and he said he would like to hear from you. So she wrote from Ohio a long letter at Christmas to him in Minnesota.

Z: OK, while she was in college in Minnesota?

R: She was in Ohio.

Z: OK, while she was in Ohio; *he* was in Minnesota. At least two of the children were scattered around the country. He was off by himself; that's an enormous kind of—

R: It's really scattered—scattered family relationships.

Z: And the man is in his early 50s, a rather critical age for a sense of being a person and being—

R: A success?

Z: Well, whatever. Being a success in some—

R: Fulfilling some of his life's goals? He doesn't even finish a year because—

Z: Because he becomes ill. That's interesting. So he comes back to Philadelphia and somehow hooks up with a church in a job which—Does it have much prestige?

R: He's manager in a church on the Main Line which is a rather good church. I don't know how good a manager. I don't know how much prestige there is in management.

Z: Is there a sharp drop in income?

R: Yes, about half.

Z: Half of what he was getting. He is not retirement age, so a drop of that much would have to mean a lot to the man. It would kind of—

R: A slap in the face; a blow to his pride, certainly.

Z: A judgment. Men being what they are, that has to be a judgment.

R: How about a woman?

Z: Women may not have that judgment leveled against them so much. Maybe that's a sex bias, but I don't think so.

R: The daughter sounds like it's happened to her.

Z: Yes, she may have been sensitized to the father's situation and felt particularly bad because she could not help him in that. There is something between father and daughter.

R: A very strong relationship between father and daughter.

Z: OK, we have an interesting family situation there, and I think you've been carrying on those interviews nicely; the exchange is nice. There are some things that come to mind. The engagement issue is not an issue any longer, so you're through the engagement. The engagement is simply the first critical incident. See, I really think of family therapy as composed of a series of what I call critical incidents. Now other people might ordinarily use critical incident to connote something involving a crisis event. Well, it can be used that way. But what I mean is that the engagement, getting together with the family to decide what you're there for, is a critical incident; and it has indeed a *time*, a number of minutes or hours in which you have to reach some type of conclusion with the family as to what you're doing there together. The presenting problem was the girl's recent episode in which she was hospitalized. It sounded like a crazy diagnosis, but we won't go into that. She frightened people enough that it appeared she needed to be in a hospital for a while. She reintegrated when she was returned to a more controlled environment at home and maybe away from some of the great storm and stress at school. But now, I don't think that symptom is why you

Z: see families; that is not for me the basis. It brings families into your presence. They come to you because some member has shown some type of troublesome behavior or conduct, and there is the belief in some members of the family or some referring source that the family needs family therapy. But family therapy is not for the symptom.

R: You mean that's just a precipitating incident?

Z: That's why they come into the meeting; you get together on that basis. Why *you* see them, I think, is different. Of course eventually you like to see, as any good therapist does, any presenting symptoms improved. But that isn't really why you're exchanging with them. I think that the engagement, the goal of the engagement, is to discover why you're together. You haven't formed the basis for family therapy just on the basis of the presenting symptom. Why are you seeing them? If you're seeing them and are content with some kind of improvement in the girl's behavior, in my judgment it's not enough. The term I use is pathogenic relating. I'm very interested in family history. We've been talking a little bit about history in your discussion: the interesting correspondence between the father and daughter's affect states; the interesting symptom shared between father and daughter. The way the mother is used like a kind of telephone between the generations. The way the other two children are keyed in closely to the mother. The kind of down, depressed, defeated affect of both father and daughter; and the father's rather disturbing work history. All of these are interesting bits of information. But I want to know, in coming to some conclusion as to why I'm seeing the family, what is it they are doing in my *presence* as I get to know them that is destructive to their welfare? Now *that* you haven't yet talked about, and maybe you can talk about that. What is it, as I talk to the people, what is it that they're doing with me and with each other that I see repeated in various forms and that is, in my judgment, harmful to their inter-relating or to their relating to outsiders or to their attitude toward life? What are they doing with me? Do they shut me out in such a way that I feel uncomfortable or unable to raise certain issues? Do they do this with the children? What is the nature of the control? Know what I mean by control: how do they get such a sort of lukewarm emotional context, when you know damn well there's a lot cooking, let's say in the daughter and in the father? Who turns the father down so low emotionally, for example, that he has to sit there rigid and remote? I suspect it's his wife. She has enormous control here. She looks nice, she looks pleasant, she looks concerned; and she is, I suspect she is. But what is there about

Z: what is going on among these people, that no matter how nice it may
     appear some people are suffering unduly from that regime? My hint
     would be to you, how do you feel about it? What questions do you feel
     you can or cannot raise, because directed against you as therapist will
     probably be the same system directed toward an outsider? You're still
     an outsider. My suspicion will be they will do with you what they've
     done with themselves over a period of years, and you may find yourself
     at some point saying, why in the hell is it so hard for me to talk about
     sex? Or the thought may strike you, why do I always have to talk in
     such a low, controlled voice? Why am I doing that? Or why am I
     concerned about Mr. So-and-so's state of mind so that I have to treat
     him very carefully, gingerly? Now these to me would be cues that you
     are responding to the system, participating in it, maybe evoking it. In
     other words, much of the interaction looks nice, calm, moderated, con-
     trolled, and there may be nothing wrong with it. But for the purpose of
     the family therapist, I think you have to draw some conclusions and
     make some judgments about that interaction; and with *you* in it be-
     cause you're a participant in that interaction. So I wouldn't at all be
     satisfied with the notion that the daughter is improving or not im-
     proving, or that you're getting the family history and you see some
     interesting associations between the symptom patterns of various mem-
     bers. It's all to the good; it's very nice. And when you write up this
     case, you would want to put that in. But all I'm concerned about is,
     what are these people doing with me in this room now? And why am
     I reacting to them in such a way that I can or cannot say certain things?
     Why are they reacting to each other in such a way that certain things,
     certain issues, are not raised? Who shuts whom up? Who silences whom?
     Is there an implicit threat that if something breaks down, someone will
     go crazy? Some families are engaged in an either/or business; there are
     no gradations of disorganization. The basic message is, we are either
     controlled here or we're crazy. We are either conformist or crazy. We
     are either one extreme or the other. In other words, the flexibility in
     the family is limited. So that when the girl, let us say hypothetically, is
     involved in a situation which is stressful, which may be very provoca-
     tive sexually, she becomes totally disorganized. There aren't any grada-
     tions in the conduct. So, what is the nature of what I call pathogenic
     relating, which doesn't have to do with the history? What do I think
     they're doing with me in the interview? It's an additional burden on
     the therapist to be personally responsive to the process. It's an addi-
     tional burden because you're more involved in it than you would be
     if you handled it from the other framework, which is the more his-

Z: torical one. The historical facts are relevant, and they should give you a lot of hints as to the nature of the pathogenic relating within the family. You don't know what goes on outside of interviews; when they leave you, you don't know what goes on. Now if you don't see the pathogenic relating directly, you've got to try to provoke it. If everything looks too good, you've got to find some way to make things look not so good. So you learn all kinds of tactics to provoke, annoy, stimulate, tease, to elicit what it is desired to keep from you.

R: Doesn't it concern you at all if you find families that are only too willing to stick with you; in the sense that perhaps you're promoting the pathogenic relating?

Z: The mere wish to stick with you is neither good nor bad. I do not have the experience, and don't think there are many in this field who have the experience, that a family therapy term of a year or two or three, simply in terms of time, is of any significance. There may be cases, and I have had those cases as well, in which a family will stay with you as long as you so desire, but you must make a judgment about time. There is a point beyond which you are simply functioning as a dependency object; an object on which to depend. Change is not involved. You must come to a point where you precipitate an end to the relationship. At which point you may get some interesting changes occurring, because you find people struggling to hold on to that relationship. In that context some very interesting and beneficial changes can occur. You get families wanting to hold on to it, and in wanting to hold on to it they present little gifts to the therapist. It's a manipulation on the part of the family, but manipulation is life. I hope that doesn't come as a shock to any of you at this point. It is a perfectly normal manipulation of families with respect to outsiders who have become meaningful and useful and helpful. The therapist must make use of that in the interest of the work with the family. He doesn't do it out of some grand desire to be simply manipulated or controlled.

R: Do you think all of the families that you see are capable of change? For instance, let's say that there is such a family that you are describing that is dependent and makes gestures to keep you involved with them because they feel that they will not function well without you. Do you feel then that they are capable of making a change; that they can function well without you?

Z: After all, as a therapist what are you there for? Are you simply a source of support? That is not my definition of therapist. Implicit in the defi-

Z: nition has to be the notion of change. You are not there as a family friend primarily, are you? I don't think so.

R: No, but what we see in the outpatient department are people who return. Maybe 10 years ago they had a break and now they are having another one. And they go back and forth you know over the years, maybe twice a year to the clinic to visit; and it seems as if they need something in their life. And to demand that they change or you terminate with them, I don't know if that's realistic; that's all I'm saying. Is that realistic?

Z: Now when I'm talking about termination, I'm talking about having developed a relationship with the people and having become meaningful in their lives. Now the episode you're suggesting, well, I'm not quite sure what you are suggesting there. But remember also that there are many other therapeutic agents, thank goodness, that function in society. People like caseworkers and people like counselors of a variety of types. There are all kinds of programs that are useful and can be used as supportive agents. They may also be change agents too. You've got to have the sense from the patient or family or whatever, that they need you; they need you for something. However, simply being needed is not enough in therapy because it doesn't produce, of itself, a change. It is a requisite; it is necessary but not sufficient. It is necessary to be needed. It provides a foundation potentially for change, but it isn't change. And as a therapist I think you've really got to think about how you want to be seen by people; what gives you gratification, and what gives you pleasure. There's some difference undoubtedly here between male and female therapists. It's a problem: and if you think sex has nothing to do with your functioning as a therapist, it's nonsense, of course it does. It's a powerful conditioner in the same way that race is; in the same way that your religious background is. If you think these are neutral characteristics, that's a terrible mistake. You'll become aware of how powerful they are. You'll become aware that you can relate much more easily to some people than you can to others as patients. And you'll become aware of how much it has to do with religious background and race and sex and age.

R: How do those factors become issues?

Z: People don't listen to you—

R: Does the family therapist divulge all of this material about himself?

Z: No, but people aren't blind. They are responding to these things without telling you about them. Age, for example, is a powerful factor. I've seen young therapists go in and start preaching to older patients. Now

Z: if the patient is wise enough and has heard this before, he will play a very good game so that the young therapist thinks that he or she is being effective. And maybe the older patient will provide some little reward because it's rewarding just to be talked to, you know, even if you are talked to by some young upstart. But there is no way that you can get through to some families if you are below a certain age.

R: Well, I guess that's obvious. But I was talking more—

Z: So it would be a very wise young therapist to be very careful about preaching, or providing any directives to older people. The people won't listen to you. They may pretend to listen, but they won't be listening to you. So the wisest thing is just to say as little as possible. Of course, that's wisest in all therapists, to try to cut down the volume of your—

R: Like in the case of that 59 year old couple now that we're seeing.

Z: It's very difficult for young therapists. I think it's very difficult for a therapist who sticks out in any physical dimension. An extremely attractive person or an extremely unattractive person evokes expectations in a patient that the person may never be aware of but may limit the amount of movement possible. So if possible the ideal therapist should be neither one way or the other. They are very influential features of your functioning and you'll find in time that you simply function better with certain types of patients, and the reason why is that there is more congruity of background. We do better with people of our own background. It's an enormous problem when you have to bridge too much of a social gap or physical appearance gap or an age gap.

R: I think foreign residents must have a very difficult time doing family therapy. You know, we speak the language, we're American, and here these guys are trying to do family therapy with this handicap. They look foreign and they speak not as good English.

Z: I have heard, let's say with black families, that there's a tendency with foreign therapists to bypass some of the hang-ups between white American therapists and black patients. Of course there are enormous gulfs and terrible handicaps in white therapists working with black patients or black families. That doesn't mean that it shouldn't be done and that there aren't perfectly good techniques that can be developed, that are fruitful and have good pay-off. It means that there are fairly delimited goals involved in the work. And I think anybody who pretends differently is a bit foolish. It doesn't mean that there can't be a good outcome; it means that the outcome will be fairly delimited.

R: In your writing you seem to imply that the best results can be obtained by getting the therapist and the people as similar as possible. Do you still feel this is true?

Z: Well—

R: Religion, race, age, social background.

Z: It does neutralize some of the greatest impediments to communication and to responsiveness and trust. But let us say we have a middle-class black therapist working with a lower-class black family. Well, you have almost the same problem, because the black lower-class family will perceive the middle-class black therapist as like Whitey. And the middle-class black therapist *may* be more like Whitey than Whitey. But let's maybe return to the points raised earlier about engagement and termination. What I mean is that engagement is the first critical incident, and that change can occur within very few meetings. You can have an effect or impact on a family in one or two meetings that can be lasting. You may not be able to trace that in direct statistical terms very well; but you may discover it some months later or perhaps even years. So much of the use of the family therapist is as an agent operating within a critical situation in which stress may be high; in which there may be a lot of turmoil; in which the therapist is functioning to resolve some of that stress. It can have a very profound, lasting effect even though you have only seen that family a few times. Nobody would want to work just in that context, because being more or less middle-class type people, we are committed to the notion of lasting, durable relationships. We are bound by that notion as a result of our own up-bringing, and therefore we need for our own welfare and health as therapists situations in which we have contact with patients over a long period of time. But most of the situations you encounter will be brief, so please develop your skills with that reality in mind. You work with the engagement, you work to engage the family or couple, but also at the same time you're working to define what the engagement is about, and this involves that term pathogenic relating. What is the problem? Why should you be sitting and talking with the people, because fundamentally that is what your therapy is about. You get through the engagement; you've decided that you have some reason for being with these people. You've decided that they have some sort of problem and you've been influential in structuring what that problem is. You tell them what you think it is, and also you try to give them some notion of what you would like to work with them on. If you can reach some judgment as to how long you think it will be valuable to discuss that

Z: particular problem with them, you should give that information to them, particularly with lower-class patients because they need the structure. If you are too ambiguous, too loose, you are going to lose those people because they require more structure. That is part of their preconception of you as a therapeutic agent. Their judgment of the therapist is still too close to that of the physician. Only in the middle-class can you leave things uncertain, indefinite. You can treat therapy as a kind of learning situation, but that's only with the middle-class people. Lower-class people don't understand therapy as a learning situation. They want you to *do* something, you know.

R: There is one thing that kind of bothers me about the process of engagement. In my families that I've been seeing now for the past six months, it seems to me that you are never through the process of engagement.

Z: That's right.

R: It's a continual process and you can't define it as contract setting, fee setting, etc. It comes down to what you are actually working on in the session. Even though you may go 20 sessions and feel that you have this family engaged by all the other parameters—they're on time, they pay their fees, there appears to be change, they welcome the sessions, they appear to be working and so forth—you get to a critical incident, as you might call it, where you find out that your goals were not mutual.

Z: Exactly.

R. There is another period there where you go through another process of redefining.

Z: That's right. I'm with you on this, but I would put it a little differently. I would say that there are many critical incidents. Family therapy to me is just one critical incident after another, beginning with the engagement. Now I have to define engagement as those first few meetings in which you set the terms for the future: the future being an indefinite business, but being partly defined by the class of the family, whether it is a crisis situation, whether it is a middle-class family, whether it's a family of a certain level of disorganization, and so on—all of which influence how long that contact will be. Now you want to gear your method to that family situation. But it's quite as you said, you're really going through one engagement and termination after another; one after the other, just like in a circle. Each circle to me constitutes a critical incident. The first one is composed of your first few meetings. I'm defining it very pragmatically: the first 4 or 5 meetings, that's a critical incident. You get through that and you go on to another. You get through that one, you go on to another. Now each new critical incident

Z: raises new tensions. You may say to a family: well, now let's see, we've got to this point; these seem to me the central issues in the family; this is what you're about; this is where you are. I think it may be useful to go on, but I think we should focus on this point, this area. Now you've got that issue. They've got to decide whether they want to go on with it. You may have raised an issue with them and they may not want to go along with it. You may raise an issue that they are not prepared to deal with, and in that case you are going to lose them. You may not know you are going to lose them. You take the risk of losing them because that's in the nature of your role as a therapist. You can't have complete control in that situation. You take risks all of the time, and as you go into each critical incident you are evolving new risks; there are new risks in the situation, but that's in the nature of the therapy. Incidentally, you will never know when a family changes. Families don't change; or it may be more accurate to say there is no measure now and I don't expect there to be any measure in the future, which shows family change. Our limitation is that we must depend on the change described by someone in the family regarding some member.

R: But they really don't change?

Z: I see the concept of family change as absolutely useless.

R: I don't understand. Systems can never change?

Z: We work with those concepts, but there is no way of defining family change. There is no way. You can never see families change. You can only see and hear reports about something happening differently in the conduct of members. It's like, what is the analogy with the atoms: you can't see the atoms; you see their tracks.

R: Then there is no change, you're saying?

Z: I'm not saying there isn't any change. I'm saying that it's impossible to perceive it or probably even conceptualize how a *family* would change.

R: You can't do all of that; but there is change?

Z: There is change, but we are forced to explicate it in individual terms—that's what I'm saying. The therapist directs change; the therapist introduces change. You say to a member when you have established a level of confidence, level of trust, you say: I would like to see *this* come about. So the therapist introduces change in a very specific way. You say: I would like this to happen; I would like you to do this. Change comes about as a result of a kind of bargaining between the therapist and family members. The therapist bounces some demands off a member, and the member bounces demands back. It's out of that process

Z: that something happens because what is at issue is that relationship, the continuation of the relationship. Always the last card that we hold is, do you want this relationship? Because that's the last card in all human relationships. The threat is to the continuation of a needed relationship. It may seem to you very manipulative to do that. But all I'm telling you is, that is the basis for most human relationships; for a lot of the good things that happen in human relationships as well as many of the bad things. As therapists we simply have to become aware of that and utilize it for the benefit of the people we're working with. We are not there simply to have the relationship with patients; we are there to produce some kind of beneficial change. That's our function; that's our job.

R: What I'm having a hard time understanding is, what are the criteria that you use to pick out what the pathogenic relating is?

Z: What I refer to as silencing strategies in a family are a very pervasive form of pathogenic relating. But you have to make a judgment about what is the level of pathogenicity. They happen in all families. It's up to you as a therapist to decide how virulent is the form; how destructive? Who gets hurt the most, and is it a serious kind of hurting? Some types of noise-making in families are very pathogenic; where you hear families just make a lot of noise. Nobody gets heard; everybody's message gets garbled. This influences an individual's thinking; nobody thinks clearly in such a family.

R: Let me ask you something. You were saying a bit before that you don't see change in families, and yet when you start working with a family, one of the major tasks as therapist is to sit there and figure out what it is they are doing to you in terms of pathogenic relating.

Z: That's right.

R: And that the kinds of pathogenic relating that are going on within the family will also be directed toward you. In the course of therapy would you see less of this pathogenic relating and perhaps more health-directed relating?

Z: Yes, but in practical terms you see it only indirectly in the reported changes in symptoms or conduct. Because you can't measure, or I don't think it's likely to be able to measure, decreases in pathogenic relating. You presume that it has been decreased when you get a report about family members behaving differently toward each other or toward outsiders, or that they are doing things in a more cooperative way. You get it by indirect measures. Now let's go back again to the question about pathogenic relating. In the family reported earlier, it may be in

Z: the way they are so cool that is the problem in that family. My suspicion has to do with the way the mother is managing the situation. She seems to have a very quiet, concerned, interested way of handling all of those children and her husband. It would occur to me, is there some problem in it; does she cool everything off too much? Why is it that the children can't form more solid relationships with peers? What's being turned off there? Who has turned it off?

R: Well, you really have to guess.

Z: Of course. You're drawing conclusions. Hopefully, your guess accumulates more evidence. The moment you intervene into the system, you will find often unsuspected members of the family getting in your way; people that you would have thought were mainly on your side. Suddenly you find these people being obstructive. The system is simply trying to maintain itself. The persons may not even be aware of what they are doing. They suddenly present themselves as walls or as barriers to movement. And you've got to do something about that. By definition the system has to have stability, and if you move against the system, which is essentially to try to change it, you'll be moving against an object which has the capacity to restore itself against efforts to change its shape or contour.

R: I'd like to ask you another question about systems to make it a little clearer. It seems that what you are trying to do is identify the silencing strategy, and who is the silencer and who is being silenced.

Z: If that's the basic problem.

R: Is there something else you might look for besides the silencing strategy?

Z: The reason why I think that the silencing strategy concept is most useful to start with is that it is almost universally seen, certainly in families that we see.

R: Are you saying that it is sort of a controlling mechanism?

Z: Sure it is. Controlling mechanisms that function to impede the welfare of family members; that prevent them from growth; that prevent them from using their most constructive potential, or impair their emotional functioning. Again it moves back to the individual framework on which we must hinge results. Results are shown in terms of *individuals* in family work, not in terms of families. You may be deceived a little bit by the literature in that regard, which tells you all about how families change, but I tell you you don't see families change.

R: Well as individuals change, doesn't that create an input into the family system which changes it?

Z: Individuals are changing in family therapy in response to a person called therapist. I assume that is why you are there as a therapist with a family. It's your attempt to put change into family members. As I've said before, one of the hints also that change has occurred among members is that sometimes your own notion of what has been the problem in the family changes. In other words, when the *therapist* changes, sometimes then the family can change. When I see things differently than I saw them before, it's a clue to me that something probably has happened in the family—a possible therapeutic change has occurred.

CHAPTER 2

CONVERSATION WITH RESIDENTS: PART II

Discussion of August 29, 1973

Z: (Discussion begins with a reference to the discussion of August 22, 1973) There are a couple of things that came up in my watching the playback of last week. There is, you know, a technique which uses playback to show the family members what they look like while talking; and of course, to some people this can be a pretty profound shock. I think it's been used even with the problem of overweight. I was using the playback technique on myself.

R: I used it on a mother who had trouble relating to her daughter. It's been used with alcoholics, too.

Z: With alcoholics, right. I don't like to use it much. Even when families are videotaped, for example, I will offer them a chance to see the playback, but I don't push it. My reservation is that I don't want the people to get too hung-up by the mechanics of it. There's a tremendous fascination in most people with gadgetry, but I'm concerned about what they actually learn; where the focus of learning is, and how your role with the patient is affected by gadgetry. I generally tend to steer away from it, but I know others don't and I'd be interested in their rationale for what they're doing.

R: Isn't there a technique some psychologists and psychiatrists are using now where they videotape in their office and show it back as part of the—

Z: Oh yes, as part of the treatment process.

R: There was an article I saw last month about it; where they use the videotape right in their offices.

Z: I really have reservations about that; the same as with the audiotape recordings that we make. This surprised somebody at a meeting when I mentioned that reservation. The person thought I'd be naturally a proponent of it. I didn't know why the person came to that conclusion, but maybe there is something—

R: What are your reservations?

Z: The reservation is the dependence on the gadgetry and what it does to your role as therapist. To use this as a device, a therapeutic device, in general I'm more or less against. That may be surprising to some people, but I'm not in favor. If it's used it seems to me, even in the interviews such as we do here, we have an obligation to tell the people that they may see it in playback. But if they forget about it, I'm just as happy.

R: Then you don't think it serves any value to show people what they look like or sound like? Or how they're acting?

Z: Yes, that has some value, but I'm asking the additional question: what is it doing to your relationship with them?

R: But isn't it important they see the way they're behaving with their husband or wife or therapist? That they do things that they're not even aware of? That they raise their voice, or that they become angry? Whether they are becoming passive or withdrawn or whatever? And they are frequently surprised to see how they look. They didn't realize they were doing these things.

Z: Absolutely. The surprise—

R: And by showing them these things, it can sometimes help to correct some situations.

Z: But I'm still concerned as to what is the impact on the relationship with the therapist. The moment you involve a mechanical instrument in what you're doing, I think you have an impact. Good heavens, what is the concern generated by our videotaping today among you professional people; and what does it do in raising certain questions about *my* role? If it does it to you, why shouldn't it do more to patients? Now it doesn't have to be bad. I have learned some things from having to look at a lot of playbacks, I think, and have been surprised at some things that I've seen there. But I think it limits relationships in a way that I may not want them to be limited as a therapist. I think the same, you know, of the training device in which supervisors enter the trainee's room and give corrections in the presence of the family and trainee. I think that is very questionable procedure.

R: And walking out of the room and getting advice during the session.

Z: Yeah, that's got to do something to the family. Not to say anything about the therapist.

R: Time out!

Z: It's got to do something to the therapist.

R: Yeah, but I don't see that with the tapes. I think in some cases just the opposite of you; that it doesn't distance the therapist from the patient. The patient may feel that this fellow is really interested in helping me. He has videotape machines; he wants to show me how I look; he wants to help me. I think it could be construed as helpful by a patient.

Z: No, I don't agree with it. Those who have used the machines usually don't provide very much depth about their experience. There are some biases I have against involvements with machines because so damn much of the problem of our society has to do with the overdependency on machines.

R: You feel it's dehumanizing, I guess.

Z: That would be the basic principle. To some extent it dehumanizes the process. Now there are times when it is absolutely required for the purposes of teaching and learning, and so on. It's required that we do this type of teaching which involves machinery. But it also artificializes that learning situation, to some extent; and that is not so good most of the time. So if it's used, I would use it in a strictly limited way. But I didn't want to get hung-up on this, although I think it's an interesting issue that you hear about in the field today.

R: I think I would have to separate the teaching process from the therapeutic process. If we were out doing private therapy I doubt if any of us would want to have videotape, or microphones or anything. We would go into our own private room where we could feel comfortable, and the family or patient could feel comfortable without recording devices. But for teaching purposes I think it's valid.

Z: For teaching purposes, perhaps. Cotherapy is valid for teaching also, but it's an absurd position to say that all family therapy should be cotherapy. Thank goodness people aren't saying that any more, by and large. Because it never was done by many people.

R: Even though I think for teaching purposes it's valuable, it's limited because I don't think you can get people to be as they really are on tape. I know on the Day Program we taped one a week for 6 months, and the people met 3 times a week so they were all taped once. And that meeting was always different than the other two. Well, I agree with you about cotherapy.

Z: It's the same thing with role-playing. There's no role-playing a family. You can't duplicate what a family is. You can hire actors to do it, and they can portray some interesting things. But the feeling-tone is entirely different.

R: You would never use role-playing?

Z: For teaching purposes, it has a value. In a limited way. Even then at times things can get a little silly. I'm not sure what the actual substantial gain is. I know in meetings people seem to respond well to the simulated family.

R: Is it more an entertainment?

Z: Well you know, it is entertainment. Now that may be a slightly jaundiced view, but I find people in meetings respond very spontaneously and positively to role-playing and the simulated family technique. The actual learning they get out of it is probably near zero.

R: Then you never use role-playing?

Z: I don't. But I think there is some teaching value in it. It familiarizes people with what a family interview *might* look like if they ever sat in on one or ever conducted one—and there's a value in that. That's why we like to start trainees looking through a one-way mirror. How does this family interview differ from an individual interview, which differs from a group therapy interview, which differs from a milieu-type interview in a hospital, etc.? It's helpful to see what the damn thing looks like.

R: Are you implying that extraneous techniques in psychotherapy cause an interference with the go-between process that you talk about in family therapy?

Z: The interference is so great that I try to avoid using all of them.

R: Because this is not very unlike the thinking of analytic theory that extraneous technique interferes with transference.

Z: The basis for my thinking is not the transference issue. The basis for my thinking is that it impedes the development of the relationship of a kind that I think necessary to get things going. It displaces the effectiveness of the treatment onto gadgetry or onto special techniques such as cotherapy.

R: Well, aren't you saying you're introducing too many variables?

Z: Too many. There are enough as it is.

R: You as an individual are enough?

Z: The old rationale that you need two people because the family is stronger than you, well, I think that's pretty weak thinking. Since when are you assured that the presence of two or three therapists in weight-value is any superior?

R: Or to provide a mother and father figure?

Z: Or to provide a mother and father. Since when should therapists take such confidence in that position either; in that heterosexual model, the parental model? Not so many people are talking that way these days.

Z: There are one or two, but I think that this thinking has kind of di- minished in popularity. And also some studies have come out which concluded that once you have tried cotherapy, you don't want to do it again when you have the opportunity not to. Most people discard it after awhile.

R: Do you feel that even for training purposes cotherapy doesn't have much value?

Z: The only value it has is that. Except in the rare instance in which two therapists *can* function as one. There may be instances where two therapists can achieve that. It may be a male and female therapist where you have a clearcut hierarchy or power difference that both parties can accept. You may have a supervisor/trainee relationship where both are clear in their roles; where there isn't implicit or explicit competition over those roles. Where the male has the more structuring role in the therapy, and the female is in the more supportive role. You do need clearcut role distinction for cotherapy not to get in the way of the therapy process. But mostly it does. Now I want to go back to one of the comments that came up last week. It had to do with change. Families may change but we don't see it happening, nor has it been useful to think of things happening in those terms. Because what we usually hear about or experience in the interview is someone talking in a somewhat different way about himself and others as individuals. That for me is a specific delimitation of the therapy context. We hear about change or sometimes hear reports about different things happen- ing. People in the family are doing different things, perceiving each other differently, and acting as if these differences were true. Some- times as therapists we get a sense of the people in the family being either better or worse off than we thought earlier. As for those people who talk about family change and family systems, I have reached the point where I really don't know what they're talking about any more. The term systems has such diverse meaning today that it's almost an in- operable term. I've heard people of such diverse origins talk about the term as if it were *their* term and as if they were systems-oriented, that I just have had to conclude that it doesn't mean anything any more. We don't see these family systems change. What we see is just what happens in front of us; and to talk about it as family system change is not helpful. We are constantly involved in trying to formulate things in systems terms. I would still use the term in that specific way. I try to think about processes as occurring in a systems way, but I don't get hung up on the belief that one sees family systems *change*. All you know is what happens when you meet with the people. You don't know what happens outside.

R: Yeah, but some people have told us that what you see in that hour is a reflection of what they do in their everyday lives.

Z: It is a reflection.

R: The way they relate to each other in front of you is the way they relate to each other at home. Haven't you told us that?

Z: It depends on how you mean that. Last week I mentioned that I think people in interviews with you do replay certain processes that they've learned to play with each other over a period of years; but I don't make a hell of a lot out of that. The only thing I know is what they're doing with me in the interview. We are engaged in the process of trying to formulate what goes on in those meetings. I make as few assumptions about what goes on outside as I can. I'm forced to make some but I make as few as possible; and that's why I really don't like to talk about family change, because I don't know what the hell goes on outside interviews.

R: You prefer to talk about individual change.

Z: I prefer to talk about what I hear from the people, and what I see at that particular time I am with them.

R: And you can't call that change?

Z: I can if I draw such a conclusion about it; if I *decide* to call it change. Let's get back to clinical examples, because we are getting too philosophical here. You see a family two or three times, and one of the presenting problems, although you may not have heard of this in the first interview, is that father really is an alcoholic according to his wife. They may have come in for some other problem. Let's say a son is acting-up in the classroom. But you find out at the end of the first meeting or sometime at the beginning of the second that really the son is not such a problem. In other words, sometimes your presenting problems are not really the big problems. You find out really that what is affecting everybody much more is the father's drinking. So you say to the wife: oh, your husband drinks too much. No, she says: he's an alcoholic! So there is an exchange, a transaction. By transaction I don't mean anything terribly philosophical, I just mean by it an exchange between you and the people you are sitting together with in an interview. Here we begin to get these contradictions. The presenting problem when the school counselor sent the family in was was the son's school performance, but by the end of the first meeting we hear that a really more pervasive difficulty is the husband's drinking. His wife calls him an alcoholic. That's a problem in definition: is he or isn't he? One of many helpful things a therapist can do is explore that particular process

Z: and maybe help to revise the definition of the husband, essentially
formed by his wife who has been powerful enough to get her children
to reinforce her definition. You know, it's one thing when a husband
has this judgment leveled against him by a wife; it's another to have
that judgment leveled against him by his children. It's a reinforcement
that may indeed place the man fully in the alcoholic role. The therapist
may decide that that's a nice issue and go after it; and so a good many
sessions may be focused in and around the issue of the husband's
drinking. Who decided how much he drank? Do the children really
believe that he's alcoholic? Do they know what it means? Where did
the wife get this notion? Was her father a heavy drinker; and did she
really have the notion that if a man had three bottles of beer at night,
he was an alcoholic? Her father had three bottles of beer at night, and
he was an alcoholic because her mother told her that. You know how
these stories develop.

R: You said about low-income families that they are difficult to engage;
they're very difficult to keep in therapy and very difficult to get information from.

Z: Yes, and you don't interpret to them much. You don't use interpretation much because interpretation is assault on people who have a great
distrust of words.

R: They take it as a judgment.

Z: It's a judgment of a kind that is unacceptable. Middle-class families also
take interpretation as judgment, but it's acceptable within their value
system. With lower-class people so much is done by non-talk. Some
people describe blacks as talking in overtones, and that does seem so
true of black verbal patterns. Other ethnic groups are similar in their
distrust of words.

R: Isn't the behavior in lower-class, lower-economic families more controlled by guilt-producing situations, shameful situations; and that's
why when you sit with them and you try to appeal to their ego and
try to point out by interpretations or confrontations, there is very little
there that you can appeal to?

Z: But what about the whole concept of the trustworthiness of the spoken
word?

R: Well, I think you would be very distrustful too of the spoken word if
every time you heard it, you were made to feel guilty or ashamed or
embarrassed, or any of these overwhelming feelings.

Z: Now wait, middle-class people—

R: Middle-class people get an opportunity to get educated; to get exposed to people who have more than they do. And that does make a difference.

Z: The confidence in the sincerity of words is much greater in the middle-class. But what about where confidence doesn't exist in language; where to be told something in direct English is perceived as enormously threatening? Where your capacity to respond by alternatives, by options, is very limited in language?

R: Well, that's because the ego has been short-circuited by these overwhelming anxieties that get stirred up; by the use of this type of verbiage.

T: Well, I've noticed a curious pattern with the poverty people. Their language is definitely limited but they give covert responses many times. I was visiting a family once, and the mother got up and I figured—

R: You mean non-verbal behavior?

T: She got up and put the kettle on, and then I knew that that was acceptance. And when you hit a sensitive area, sometimes they will talk with their feet. They may just rub their feet.

Z: What would happen if you had said, "Now I see, madam, you are rubbing your feet or you're moving your feet?"

T: I could have given a nice Freudian interpretation.

R: But it wouldn't mean anything.

Z: No, it wouldn't.

R: It makes them very uncomfortable, too.

Z: You would record that observation, but you probably wouldn't say anything about it. Because interpreting those messages has a particularly deleterious effect on people who expect you not to do it. The lady probably had the intent to communicate something to you, but there is a kind of implicit agreement between the two of you that you shouldn't interpret that; you shouldn't point that out. But with middle-class people it's perfectly acceptable to do that. That's part of the middle-class game. You are a therapist with high verbal skills, and you're also taught about the value of explanation, of meaning, of duration of relationships and hidden meanings. What do you do with people in whom the expectation is that you will not use language to uncover? You were talking about silencing strategies last week. Is that all the therapist does is uncover silencing strategies? No. It is something the therapist should do among other things. When I see silencing going on among members of a family, I do try to comment on it. Now if it's a middle-class family, I will try to comment on it verbally in a fairly specific kind of interpretive way. If it's a lower-class family, I may do

Z: it not by that route, but by telling them in a more authoritarian way that the next time somebody opens his mouth he has got to get out of the room. But your work obviously isn't completed when you have disrupted a silencing strategy. No, that's just one aspect of your functioning as a therapist. You're functioning as a go-between there, in a sense. You are illuminating what goes on, of course taking into consideration the social class differences, the educational differences, and whether the family comes from the city or the country. Some rural families that come in are extremely controlled people, and you don't throw interpretations at them that are too sexy or too tantalizing because it injects too much anxiety. And we're as much concerned about controlling anxiety as anything. We're surely involved always in the question of trying to control the amount of anxiety of the people facing you; so that it doesn't interfere with the interview; so that it doesn't precipitate a premature termination.

T: I've seen several cases terminated with fundamentalists in Protestant sects because the therapists thought the goal was to explore and get to the anger; and in the communities in which these people lived, they weren't allowed to show that much anger.

Z: Let's say though, that this family that you mentioned got themselves one of the encounterist-type therapists who felt really that his mission in life was to unearth bad feelings and get them out. It would be a pretty bad situation. Often the encounterists appear not to be aware of how middle-class centered their philosophical position is. It's only with middle-class people that you can do that sort of thing with safety, with some security. They are so controlled ordinarily that to tell them to get their anger out is often a useful thing. The problem is over-control with middle-class people. With other families to give such a signal can be very destructive. You don't do it!

R: You mean strongly religious people?

Z: Strongly religious, and also lower-class ethnic people in whom the assaultive impulse may be right on the surface. Where really you're dealing with a problem of trying to stuff back some of the hostility and anger. You've got to work with the people to build *in* controls over the tendency for too high an immediate affective response to situations.

R: Obviously, lower-class families would be more likely to express themselves by doing something, like hitting each other and what not.

Z: That's true.

T: You could redirect that anger into some kind of activity of some sort; games or—

Z: That might be a good way to restructure. You would do that if you can, certainly with lower-class groups.

R: You haven't mentioned the upper-class at all.

Z: We don't see many in clinics.

R: Where do they go?

Z: I see a few in private practice.

R: I see. Then you feel as residents in training we won't be seeing much of these people. After we're finished?

Z: There aren't as many of them as the middle-class and lower-class. Now when you see them, you'll deal with them; but my experience with them in the clinic is limited. Let's go back again to what roles the therapist can take. What is that go-between role? It's a role in which you mediate exchanges among the members of the family; you try to facilitate exchanges among the people. At the same time you can interpret, but the interpretation level and direction and focus is hinged to your notion of where these people are and their readiness to hear certain types of information. So you either give or withhold information depending on what you feel they are ready for. That's one type of position, and it's a therapeutic position but it isn't the only position for the therapist. It is a familiar role for the therapist, as one who kind of sits and comments on things or interprets. Another position is what I call that of the side-taker. That is one who takes sides on positions that he has formulated during meetings. I saw one couple recently. The young husband is Jewish, an intellectualizer, also very skillful, a professional person. The wife is of Catholic origin, an intellectualizer, also very skillful. One of the problems between the two of them, although there was nothing said about this at the beginning, was that there was a failure to bridge the gap between the person coming from the Jewish tradition and the person coming from the Catholic tradition. In addition he was the only child in the family, and a boy; and she was the eldest of 5 or 6 children. The oldest daughter or son is often burdened with responsibilities over and above the other kids. There was a sharp cultural difference there. In American society, in which there is a great deal of intermarriage, there's a tendency to discount these differences. But those traditions still have powerful emotional content in them; and oftentimes the people don't realize the depth of it until a certain age. Well, this couple had about 10 years of marriage. I concluded eventually that it was a problem, and that I really didn't know how they were going to deal with it. But it certainly was a problem in their relationship; in whether they were going to stay together or not, and I said so. These are some

Z: things that influence the position of the therapist in therapy sessions. Side-taking is a very blunt and kind of homely term which exists in so many forms. We are constantly taking positions on questions, on issues. We do have to be aware of doing that; there's no way of avoiding it, incidentally. There's no way of not taking sides. A family will force you to do so even when you may want to stay neutral. That's part of the dynamics of working with families: they'll constantly push you into taking a position on an issue with which they either agree or disagree. The people themselves don't know exactly where they want you, and there's always that battling that goes on between family members and therapist as to who is to decide about such and such a position or such and such an issue. And it's in the battling that change arises. It's the constant trying of one side or the other to determine how the other should act. In that process change arises. What do I mean by celebrant? That's the third role for the therapist. Many Jewish families want a therapist to behave like a judge; many black families want him to behave like a social worker.

R: Is that different from being a mediator?

Z: It's different from being a mediator, yeah. You can shift roles; you can bounce from one role to another, and you do in the course of therapy. But there are times when families want you to function in a specific role. If you try to move out of that role, you're lost. Sometimes the only function that you'll be able to have with a family is that of celebrant. And that will be fairly delimited in time; but in a few sessions you may be able to accomplish something.

R: Do you mean like a judge presiding at a trial?

Z: Yeah. Oftentimes change has already occurred of a profound nature, and they want you to celebrate or be a celebrant of the fact that a change has occurred. The role you can play there is really to help seal something that is already underway or maybe 90 percent completed. It's like the minister signing a marriage certificate, you know.

R: Sounds like the deus ex machina.

Z: We need somebody to ritualize an event. Because people don't exactly know what's important and what's not. We know somebody got born: that's kind of important, you know; the birth of a child. You know somebody got married; now that's kind of important. Somebody died: that's kind of important. Those are highly institutionalized rituals. Everybody agrees these are important. But in most of the other things that happen to people, they don't know whether it's important. So they

Z: need somebody in that role of testifying that what happened was or was not important.

R: As a professional person you can say that? Sort of like a director of a movie or play?

Z: Not a director because that involves some other things. You're a director when you are in the go-between role because you're often channeling communication; you're often emphasizing certain issues in a family and de-emphasizing others. When you're the celebrant you are a quasi-institutional figure. You don't have to produce change because often it's already under way. All you have to do is confirm it or disconfirm it.

R: And you don't really do much about making the change?

Z: It's happened already. What they want you around for is to say: yes, it happened; or no, it didn't happen. It's therapeutic for someone special to make that judgment to people at certain moments in their lives.

PART III

INTERVIEWS WITH FOLLOW-UP

CHAPTER 1

TRUANTS FROM SCHOOL

The family presented in this chapter, and the couple presented in Chapters 2 and 3 of Part III, are included because they are rather typical of cases seen by family therapists in clinics, and because in a sense their outcomes are also typical. I like them precisely because they are *not* examples of magical cure or relief of symptoms. They are cases in which there is deep-set ambivalence with regard to family therapy. They are cases in which the therapist must maximize tenuous leverage to produce favorable change. But after all, a therapist's skill is not necessarily to be measured by the number of dramatic improvements he achieves. His skill is determined by his capacity to achieve a favorable balance of personality, style and temperament factors with a conceptual framework and technical framework that is applicable to the problem, and that has proved successful in handling such a problem.

The family described in this chapter is composed of parents with two teenage daughters who were school truants. The eighth interview, which was recorded on videotape, is presented in part, as is an interview that occurred approximately four months after termination. Therapy lasted about one year, in which there were 25 interviews. The recordings were made in 1969 and 1970.

My comments in the transcript are designated by the letter Z. The father is designated F; the mother, M. The younger daughter is D1; the older daughter, D2. The transcript was edited to improve readability.

Introductory Comments

Z: This is an excerpt from an eighth session with a family referred by the Court of Philadelphia for a 15 year old daughter in the family who had not been attending school. She had been truant from school approximately one year. Her older sister, 18 years old, was also a school truancy problem. I think it is relevant that this is a Jewish family, an upper lower-class Jewish family. We will see some of the values of this type of family expressed in the session.

The Eighth Interview (September, 1969)

F: She runs out of the room. She says, I don't want to hear it; I don't want to hear it. And she'll purposely—

D1: But first, he doesn't try to explain it. He does try to make her feel stupid. Because I know when—

Z: That's what I said.

D1: So he gets really violent. It's really dumb, you know.

Z: That's what I said.

F: You'll remember it wasn't like that in the beginning when we used to play bridge.

D1: That's true.

F: It wasn't like that at all. I remember I used to play with her. I used to laugh.

Z: I'm not saying that your wife is not fully capable of enraging you, because I think she is. But I think you are a little bit of a snob.

F: Well maybe so, but I know my shortcomings. I mean—Believe me, I don't think—

Z: Are you a snob? Intellectually, do you think you're a snob?

D1: You mean, does he have a superior attitude? Kind of. Sort of. Yeah.

Z: Does he?

D1: Yeah, but he is really intelligent.

Z: He is.

D2: Well, he can't help talking down on people.

Z: Down *to* people.

D1: Well, with some people you just have to talk down.

F: I respect Diane's boyfriend because I think he's got a lot of intelligence. I mean, we don't agree. If somebody's got a cause, I can respect it. You know what I mean? But if somebody's real ignorant, or something like that, and they start acting intelligent and don't know what it's all about, then you might say I am a snob then. Because that's true—

Z: You're saying something, but I'm not quite getting what you're putting in words.

D1: I think it's that he thinks somebody who has formulated opinions, that can tell you why they have these formulated opinions, will sound rational to him; then he'll have respect for them.

Z: But your wife—

D1: Unless of course they're reactionary or conservative.

Z: Your wife has no opinions?

F: My wife? She has opinions but she won't discuss them. She won't— She would rather—

Z: She's too emotional?

F: Too emotional, yeah. You see the way I'm talking to you now. I know I'm raising my voice. I know—She can't stand that, you know.

Z: Yeah.

F: I can't help it either.

M: It just doesn't go that far.

Z: How far does it go?

M: (after long pause) Well, he's very nervous too, and it goes to the point where he gets so nervous that he can't even talk.

F: Yeah, well that's true. Well, I don't know whether you noticed or not but I'm a stutterer. Of course I can talk for days and nobody would— Many people don't even know that I stutter. But if I get emotionally upset, I can't say what I want to say. And when I was a child I was a terrible stutterer.

M: And I would always tell him to stay quiet and talk quietly and say it, but he keeps—I can't stand it.

Z: You can't stand it? What is it that you can't stand? You know, you have said that many times.

M: When people get all that worked up over a lousy bridge game, or whatever else.

F: Well, whatever I do I like. I play hard. To me to enjoy a game of bridge it has to be—I can't stand when they start to sing or listen to the radio or something like that. I enjoy the game. By playing hard, whatever I do that's the way it was. I played ball in the street. Whatever it was. It didn't mean anything. Nobody made any money on the game, but I wanted to win. It's the same way.

M: Competitive.

F: It's the same way. It's the only way you can enjoy it.

D1: Capitalist! (laughter)

Z: You've been hard on your wife though in that way.

F: Perhaps, but it's because—

Z: Because she can't take that. She can't take that too well.

F: Well, I can't take things too well either. And especially now, I don't want to—

Z: (to mother) Did he ever frighten you by his blowing up like that? (pause) Are you afraid of him a little bit?

M: No, I'm not afraid of him.

Z: What do you feel when he blows up? (to father) What are you laughing at?

D1:   He's not laughing.

F: I'm just thinking, I know she's not afraid of me.

M: Oh, do you want me to be?

F: No.

Z: Well, what I'm trying to get at is, I think you have turned your wife off almost completely. And turned her in on herself. And I think it would be helpful to have her not so turned off; you'd be better off, frankly. But now whether she'll allow you to do that or whether we can do anything with her here, I don't know. She's angry and bitter. Is that true?

M: No, just upset.

Z: Upset? All right, you're upset. But I think she's upset because she's never been able to get through to you, and she probably feels at times that she is dealing with a child.

M: (in tears) I just can't talk about anything.

Z: Well you see, I'm talking for you. I'm trying to put it into words; and if I'm wrong let me know, will you? I want to ask a little bit about last week. What happened? The terrific mix-up, whether you should show up for this videotaping or not.

D1:   OK, well I'll explain it to you. She found out she had an appointment.

Z: Who's she?

D1:   My mother. She called and cancelled it and she told us she cancelled the appointment, and that we were not supposed to go. We weren't supposed to go—(laughs) Oh, never mind.

D2:   That we weren't supposed to go.

Z: Who's we?

D1/D2: All of us.

D1:   So, anyway—

Z: What appointment was it?

D1:   For the taping.

Z: For here?

D1:   Yeah, so anyway I was talking to my sister and I said that maybe we should go anyway, you know, without her; and that maybe you would like us to come anyway. And my mother said no, the whole thing was

D1: cancelled and we shouldn't show up. So me and her stayed up all night talking and then at 12 o'clock in the afternoon she woke me up and said, well it was time to go, and—(laughs)

Z: Who is she?

D1: The organism that is married to my father. (laughs)

Z: Oh, this is your mother!

F: Maybe she can tell you more, I don't know. Anyway, when she went in to wake them up they had only been sleeping a few hours. So they were in no condition to go. And I didn't feel any too well. I didn't feel too good last week.

M: So then in the morning I called and I found out that they could come; and then they weren't ready to come. They had hardly slept.

D1: But that night you had told us the whole thing had been cancelled and that we shouldn't go.

M: Oh, that was earlier.

D1: It was at night. I thought that you'd know because you told—

Z: Was that your husband, then, that you talked to and then you cancelled? Something had happened the day before?

F: The only thing that happened was that she decided that—You remember that she had to go to this—

D1: Then the secretary told us that it was cancelled.

Z: The secretary? Did she? My secretary?

D1: Yeah. She said, if we couldn't come she would cancel it.

Z: Well you said you couldn't come, for some reason. It was because you had some other appointment. Well it was really confusing. And to me it was just an example of how the family just gets everybody else all screwed up.

F: Oh, we didn't try to avoid it.

Z: No, I didn't say that.

F: It just so happened that she'd remembered the other appointment and that's what screwed everything up.

Z: What have these girls been up to this last week? Other than staying up until 8 o'clock in the morning.

F: That seems to be the biggest problem, if you want to call it that. They keep very irregular hours, you know.

Z: Well you and I are going to try something new in family therapy, you know that? We're going to get two paddles, big ones; and the

Z: next time these kids stay up that late, I think we're going to let them have it. I think maybe they'll call the police in on us; you think that?

D2: Oh no, we wouldn't do that.

Z: We'll go to jail for that?

F: I don't think I could hit them with a paddle. (laughs) I know I couldn't do that. I know I can't.

Z: You're going to let me be the bad one?

D2: You couldn't hit us; you're an outsider.

Z: I couldn't get away with it?

D2: No you can't.

F: Sometimes, you know, when she worries me—

D2: *He* could. (signifying her father)

Z: If I had their approval, maybe this would help with the police. They wouldn't bother me. I'm bigger than you; I could handle you, I know that.

D1: But I'm stronger than you.

Z: No, no.

D1: How do you know?

Z: I know, believe me you're not. Oh, no. Would it be all right if I did that one of these times?

M: Do you think that would be an answer?

Z: Well, it would help me. I would feel better if I were able to whack them every time they disobeyed me.

F: You would have to be at the apartment. I mean, how could you— (laughs)

Z: Well not here, you wouldn't be here. But upstairs. We'd have the nurses around, and then if there was any blood or anything, we'd be able to clean it up all right. There wouldn't be any lasting harm. They might be mad at me for a while.

D1: No, we wouldn't be.

Z: If they didn't like it I would probably get, you know—accept the fact that they didn't like me.

D1: No, we wouldn't *not* like you.

Z: It wouldn't—

D1: No, we would understand.

Z: I wouldn't want you to understand. I wouldn't want—

D1: No, we would.

Z: I wouldn't want you to understand. It wouldn't make that much difference to me. I would feel better if I could do that.

D1: Yeah, but you would be doing it for a completely unrelated reason. You'd be doing it just to get out your frustrations.

Z: No, I'm not that frustrated. I would be doing it, I think, to—

D1: You wouldn't be doing it to change anything.

Z: To establish a rule. I think that's maybe the idea. Is that also true of you?

M: Well, what has to be done?

Z: I can't spell it out in exact terms. I have not really seen you that many times. As I was saying before, only six or seven times. But whatever has to be done, are you on my side or not?

M: I'd have to know what—

Z: Well, you know that I'm the doctor. I'm trying the best for them.

D1: You haven't known us long enough to make your diagnosis.

D2: Just because you're the doctor—

D1: You're being very unfair.

Z: I'm not asking you; I'm asking your mother.

D1: Why don't you just take them and discuss it with them and leave us at home? We don't have any minds, do we?

Z: Sometime I'll probably do that.

D1: Well, we don't have any minds; so you might as well.

Z: When I decide that it should be done.

D1: Well, you might as well do it now.

Z: I didn't decide that yet. What did you reply to that; what I said?

M: I said I would have to know what you were anticipating.

Z: Well then you see, I'll have to move you. You shouldn't be seated over there; you should be seated over here with them. (the girls laugh)

D1: Why don't we go to war? Those two against us two.

Z: Who's going to set the rules here? You called last week and I expected you in. And first you broke the appointment; then your husband broke it; and then somebody remade it; and then somebody else broke it. And nobody sets rules. Is that unfair?

F: I can't understand where you said I broke it. We were all set to come the day before.

Z: So who decides whether you come or you don't come. Who decides that?

F: Well, first of all I thought you wanted us all together.

Z: Right. But who decides whether you come here for meetings or not; when a meeting has been scheduled?

F: I guess we all decide together.

M: We all do.

Z: Are you going to let this girl decide? (indicating older daughter)

D1:   She's here, isn't she?

Z: Whether you come to the meeting or not?

D1:   I'm human.

D2:   She's here, isn't she? If she didn't decide to be here, she wouldn't be here.

Z: I know that.

D1:   You're not aware of that.

Z: Are you going to let this girl decide whether you should be here or not?

M: It's something we agreed on. All of us.

Z: Yeah, but you don't have an equal vote. My understanding is, you're the parents. I think your vote is more than equal. That's my understanding.

F: I don't rule the authority in the house. As far as that's concerned, neither does my wife.

Z: The kids do.

F: Well, they don't tell me what to do either! (the girls laugh)

M: I like to tell everybody what to do, but nobody listens.

Z: Well, I think that's a good description of what happened. That's why I say: somebody's got to use a paddle, and I don't know when or how it's going to happen; but I think that something like that has got to happen. Somebody's got to lay the law down—in a nice way.

D1:   No, it doesn't matter if it's in a nice way.

Z: Now if I laid the law down to you, would you be unhappy?

D1:   I just wouldn't accept it no matter how you made it sound.

Z: Well, all right. I don't know if we have too much time left on this thing, but I'm glad we got together. And (to father) congratulations on your birthday. I hope somebody gets a cake or something for this evening. Or you go out or you do something.

F: Well just adding on, we'll put it one way: they are not juvenile delinquents.

Z: I didn't say they were.

F: But they just resent authority.

D1: That's not true.

Z: See, my opinion is they are too good to waste. I don't want to see that waste.

F: That's right.

Z: So I'd be prepared to do whatever has to be done to see that they didn't go to waste.

D1: That's our decision if we want to waste ourselves.

Z: No, it's not your decision.

D1: Yes it is.

Z: I say it isn't.

D1: If we're too good to waste, then we're good enough to make a decision.

D2: A person should be able to determine what—

Z: See, these people exist; whether you like it or not. (signifying the parents)

D1: Who said they don't? Of course they exist. We exist, and we're not—

Z: They're your parents. They exist and they have a role in society. And I say they should play that role. And you should accept it.

D1: Even if they're not capable of playing it?

Z: They are capable; more than you think. All right, let's stop for today.

F: OK, let's sing happy birthday to me. (laughs)

Z: I wouldn't mind. I've forgotten the song, myself.

Commentary

Z: Let's say a word or two about the interview, which I said was the eighth session. One sees the weakened lines between the generations. It is a little confusing as to who is parent and who is child. When the therapist attempts to step in as a kind of parent figure, hoping to strengthen the boundary lines between the generations, he triggers considerable resistance on the part of all members. They're all resistant to anybody who proposes to change the status quo. So a great struggle ensues as to what the change shall be, and the therapist engages in a great many maneuvers to try to shift the balance from what is typical for the family to one that is, at least in my estimate there as therapist, more hopeful for the future. Now that is the eighth session and there were 25 meetings with this family in a period of about a year; or just a little under a year. The state of the family on entry into the treatment was depressive. I think that it is fair to say that it was depressive. The girls were staying up all night; they

Z: were not getting their rest. They were not engaged in many of the daily activities or *learning* activities that we consider normal for girls of their age. I think again it is fair to say that there was a normalizing trend during the 25 meetings. Certainly the depressive atmosphere of the family diminished. There was better feeling between parents and children, and a little bit more clarity as to who was what: who was parent and who was child. It terminated at that point for a number of reasons, and I don't want to go into them here. But approximately four months after termination I learned via one of the local training schools that the older daughter, the 18-year-old, had made application there for their program. In getting in touch with them I learned to my surprise that the younger daughter was already in that program. She had begun it. It was a kind of work-training program, also including some kind of educational curriculum, which of course had been one of the practical goals of the therapy—to return the girls to some type of educational scheme and also some type of daily routine. So upon learning this I asked the family for a follow-up session.

Follow-up Interview (July, 1970)
Four Months After Termination

Z: Now it's been four or five months since I saw you last. What has been happening? I want to hear from each of you what has been happening in that time.

D1:   It's just like nothing bothers me.

Z: Is that good?

D1:   No, but I'd have to say I think it is better than how I was before—

Z: Well, the difference was that you were playing some kind—Or maybe playing isn't the right kind of word. But like you were *being* some kind of person. I don't know quite what you're saying.

D1:   Not being able to live up to certain people's standards who were important to me.

Z: Is there an example of that? What kind of person?

D1:   Well, for one I was very worried about making my father happy.

Z: Is that not such a worry any more?

D1:   Oh, I don't have to worry about it any more, because, like, I've been trying very hard to communicate with them.

Z: Since when?

D1: Well, I'd say in the last couple of months more than ever. And I feel that I have.

Z: You do?

D1: I feel that I really have. And like even though I'm not really the way he wants me to be, I feel that he's happier that I'm happier; and like he doesn't need me to do the things that he used to need me to do. Like he doesn't need for me to work. Working now is just like a financial thing. Like if it wasn't for the financial part of it he wouldn't bother me about working or going to school or anything. I could just do it if I wanted to. I'm not saying working isn't something I want to do, I just mean that he has changed in that way.

Z: (directed to older daughter) In the last few months, what's been going on? Nothing? You have nothing to say? Nothing has been happening? You've got a sun tan.

D2: It's a burn.

Z: A burn? Well, I wanted to make it sound nicer. Nothing has been happening that you can fill us in on?

F: She might learn to stay out of the sun, that's one thing.

Z: Other than that, no dramatic incidents?

M: Everything is still the same around the house.

Z: Around the house things are still the same: just as they were? Have either of you, one or the other of you, decided who causes most of the trouble? Which of you parents? (the girls laugh)

D1: It's like, her reaction to him. It's not what you call actually causing trouble; but she reacts to him in a way that causes trouble.

Z: What is it in her reaction that is so bad? Have you figured that out?

D1: When she decides to act as if he doesn't exist.

Z: She shuts him out entirely?

D2: To the extreme of like not saying a word to him, or she wouldn't answer because he was in the room and he would hear what she would say. But it's like the way he is that causes that in her; she's afraid to really say something, I guess.

Z: Then the status of today is deceptive, isn't it? Because last night— when was the last time you went out with each other? (directed to parents)

F: You mean before last night?

D1: You went to a show, Dad.

F: A show? When?

D1: Remember? Millie gave you tickets.

F: Yeah, but I think we went out before then.

M: No, that was before Father's Day.

F: Father's Day we went out and had a nice time.

Z: Both of you went out on Father's Day? When is Father's Day?

D1: The beginning of June.

F: About the third Sunday in June, wasn't it?

Z: Well then, that was just last month? You had a nice day then.

M: Yeah, I know. But in between there—

Z: In between it was pretty sad? (laughs)

F: You see, we're different. I'm a constant worrier about things. I worry about the financial situation. She doesn't worry about that. I worry about where the kids are, and she doesn't worry about that. The two of us are in constant conflict there, you know? She doesn't worry and I worry.

M: No, that isn't it.

Z: All right, where are the kids now? When you were coming in they were staying up till all hours of the night. I take it that you are still— I certainly don't expect that either of you have stopped doing that, except now it may be harder because you have to get up in the morning.

D1: No, it's no harder.

Z: No harder. You can still stay up all night? That's amazing. Well, maybe you'll stop that later. How about you? Is this every day, every night?

D2: No, it's not every night. Periodically. I have periods where I can't sleep at night.

Z: Yeah, you both have that trouble.

D1: We're hardly ever out late. Like we have these two friends who have to be in at 12 o'clock.

Z: Oh, they have to be in at 12?

D1: Well these boys, these college guys, they have to be in at 12 o'clock. (laughs)

F: Maybe things have been a little better because lately they've been going with a better brand of boys.

D1: We are not.

Z: What are you looking unhappy about? You didn't like what he said?

D2:   Well, I think it shows a lack of awareness about what our worlds are like.

Z: What is the lack of awareness?

D2:   Well, he seems to feel that these guys are like, well, that we can handle them. But he thinks if they were older, we'd be in big trouble.

Z: I don't know, maybe you've got a good solution here. You think these boys are OK. Your father thinks they maybe are homosexuals; so that doesn't bother him any more. So you're happy.

D1:   It's his attitude toward other guys. We go out with a guy and for some reason they don't act like when we're with these two. They think that they know so much more than us and we're going to believe all their lines.

D2:   Like, really *serious* people he worries about. People that don't mouth-off all the time. We can handle these two because they act like clowns, he thinks.

Z: You don't like serious people?

F: Some people I just don't know. I don't think my daughters aren't up to them in brains or anything like that. Physically they are not strong enough and something may happen.

Z: Well, what do you think about the boys?

F: They say they don't stay out real late with them because they have to be home at a certain time.

Z: (directed to mother) What do you think about the boys?

M: I guess I like them.

D1:   Don't you like them?

M: Yeah, I like them; but I've liked other ones too.

Z: What have you been doing the last few months, yourself?

M: What have I been doing? I've been getting up.

Z: Getting up? Sometimes that's an achievement!

M: (referring to younger daughter) She would be up or she would get up soon after I did; so we could stay and talk and maybe she would want a cup of coffee or tea and I would give it to her.

Z: What about meals? Are they as hectic as they used to be? Do they exist?

D1:   No, they don't exist.

Z: And I worked so hard to get you people to have at least one meal a week together, and you completely ignored what I told you. I feel very useless when you do that to me.

M: Well, one reason is because nobody seems to want to eat at the same time.

D1: And he has to wake me up and I'm already up. But he has to make sure I'm up. He should have enough confidence in me to know that I'm up. You know, I just don't like the idea that he comes in and says, are you ready? I don't like that.

D2: It's the attitude. I don't like that.

Z: You don't like the attitude?

F: Nobody likes the attitude of anybody who has to wake them up.

M: Even when I had to go to work at four o'clock in the afternoon, he had a funny way of getting me up.

D1: Now today was the first day that I didn't go in, right Dad? I was sitting in my room and I was up, you know.

F: You were up but it was late.

D1: Well you could have come out and said what time it was. But you come out and say, aren't you going in today?

M: Yeah, you always do it the most pessimistic way.

F: She was still sleeping. She had to be in 15 minutes ahead of you and you were already late.

D1: You don't know anything about it. We were both on time.

F: When you were supposed to be there at quarter after eight and you didn't start out until quarter after eight, how could you be on time?

D1: I was on time. You see, I know what time is acceptable for me to come in and you don't.

F: I so want this thing to succeed, not because of the financial end of it, but because—

D1: No, *because* of the financial thing.

Z: Is that really true?

D1: Of course, because of the financial thing. He even told me the other day; because he's worried about being destitute.

F: Yeah. We had a little money but it's going down the drain. It has to go down because, what can I make three nights a week working? I don't want to have that feeling where I have to rely on welfare. My wife don't give a damn. She goes with a girl that's on welfare and she wants to be in the same position she is.

Z: I thought your wife worked for the Internal Revenue.

F: She blew that; she claims she didn't, but I think she did.

Z: Did you blow that?

M: No, not really.

F: That's what bothers me too.

Z: What happened?

M: Nothing happened. Just a slowdown in the work and we were laid off.

D1: Like she went there and she's working for the Internal Revenue, and she's very into the Peace Movement. So then she puts stickers all over the wall. You know, like peace stickers and everything. (laughter)

F: Here she is laughing about it and we're discussing it.

M: The young woman that was sitting beside—working beside me said that she heard some of the big shots talking that they had the FBI in and looking for who did it.

Z: You put the stickers on the wall?

M: But is that such a horrible thing to do?

F: It's enough to make you lose the job.

M: No, it isn't.

D1: Yes, it is.

M: No, it isn't.

F: (directed to therapist) Do you think so or don't you think so? I'll ask your opinion. If they would find out that she was putting stickers all over the wall?

D1: Maybe they can't legally fire you for that, but they'll put you on the bottom of the list to ever come back.

Z: Why did you put the stickers on the wall?

M: I thought the thing needed advertising.

F: I even pleaded with her when she first went back to work. I was happy because I thought that maybe we'd get out of this financial rut.

M: It had nothing to do with it.

F: You say it didn't, but I say it did.

M: I know there is something else behind it.

D1: Well, that doesn't matter. It's just the fact that you did it.

M: OK, I did it.

F: The fact remains that she wouldn't listen to me just once. The fact that she just doesn't realize what just kind of financial situation we're in, you know?

M: Yes, I do.

F: No you don't! You don't care if we're in the same position as your friend.

M: She's in a better position than we are.

Z: The lady who is on welfare?

M: Yeah, she is.

F: That's what you want; to be on welfare? I don't want to be on welfare.

M: Well I can't help what you don't want.

Z: (directed to girls) You know, you're going to have to live in spite of your parents. Right?

D1:   How true.

Z: I think it's true. I hope—If anything came out of that therapy experience, I hope it was that awareness that you've got your lives to lead and you can't reform your parents, you know. You can't make them into new people. You've got to live your lives and you cannot do otherwise. I certainly would not want you to do otherwise. You are entitled to live your own lives without being responsible for your parents' lives, or for every helpless person. Actually if the treatment meant anything to you, I hope it meant that you're responsible for your own lives. And I mean the same for your parents. I don't like to see you in this kind of impasse with your husband, but I don't expect that to change very much. Except you have the possibility to make the change; and if you really wanted to work at it you probably could make a change somewhere. Now the steps you've taken I think are very promising. I'm very proud of both you girls, and I'm not too terribly unhappy with you parents. I think you're still alive and you're working and you're trying. You're failing in many ways with each other but then, you're still trying.

M: Well, I've decided to live even if he doesn't want to.

Z: Good! You go ahead and live even if he doesn't want to. You're entitled to that; you're fully entitled to that. I approve of that and I think that's great and I want the girls to do the same thing. All right, we probably still have a little while left on the videotape and I don't know exactly what we should do with it.

F: Tell jokes? (laughs)

M: Oh, let's talk about the pictures we took.

Z: No, let's not do that because I want to review in my mind what we— During the time you were coming in here, what did you think was going on? What were we doing here? Was it a complete waste of our time?

F: We were trying to iron out problems. We were seeking help. I realize it was a hard nut to crack; but it helped.

D1: It was something that was doing some good while we were doing it. It couldn't go on forever; therefore, it couldn't have any lasting, really good lasting effects, so far anyhow.

D2: No.

Z: None of you do see any lasting effects of the treatment?

D2: I think that's because we're not capable of just sitting down and talking about our feelings and what's happening in our family. We have to be forced to.

Z: Yeah. And when you're not forced to, then you go your own ways, right? Do you agree with that?

M: Well, I have a low breaking point.

Z: A low breaking point?

D1: Well, what she means is that it's very hard for her to talk about things without crying all over.

Z: Is that what you mean by that? How come she can express it better than you can?

M: Because I feel that way now.

Z: Yeah, well that's true. But you see it would be better if you could say that. It would take the burden off your daughter.

M: Well, she doesn't have to say it.

Z: No, it's true she doesn't have to say it, but she's so damn used to saying it! If you had said it, she wouldn't have to say it.

M: Was it necessary to be said?

D1: The question was asked.

M: Well, I gave him the answer to it.

Z: Of course *you* interrupted. I didn't really ask you. (directed to younger daughter)

D1: OK, I'm sorry.

Z: No, you don't have to be sorry because that's the way things are.

D1: I'm the only one in the family that is capable of expressing.

F: She has a way with speech.

Z: Oh yes, that's absolutely true. I'm very much aware of that. She talks for all of you and she's good at it. That's one of the problems, isn't it? She's pretty good at it.

M: I don't think that's a problem. I think that's good for her. Not to the point that she should worry about it, because she can talk.

Z: *I* said it was a problem. She's so good at it that you let her do that and she takes on the burden of explaining the family to, let's say, me.

M: Is that a burden?

Z: I think it's a burden.

M: Do you feel burdened?

Z: Ask me!

M: No, I'm asking her.

Z: *I'm* bothered by it. *I* think it's a burden.

D2: Why does it bother you?

Z: Because it's like being a psychologist or a therapist. If I were to do it it wouldn't be so bad, because I would get paid for it, it's my job. But this little girl, it's not her job to explain everybody to everybody else.

M: No, it's not her job, but it makes it easier on her to be able to say something.

Z: It makes it easier on you!

M: No now wait, if we all sat here and didn't say anything, she would feel uneasy. The fact that she can express it makes her feel better.

Z: Yes, I'm not saying that it doesn't have some positive things because she can do this and everybody accepts her doing it. And I think that within reason it's not such a terrible thing. But it has at times gotten out of hand and it's too much of a burden. Why you let her talk for you all the time I've never quite understood.

D2: I can express myself at times; but when I'm under pressure to say something, I can't.

Z: Yeah, I understand that. Now I asked you about the therapy itself, and I assume that everybody feels that not too much came out of that while you were here. Is that correct?

D1: No. While we were here there was some good from it.

Z: While you were here there was some good. Afterwards things sort of dropped off. Did you feel while you were coming in also that there was some benefit for you?

F: No, not too much. It was a way of unburdening myself. But I don't think too much was accomplished, no.

Z: Now, how about your reaction to the therapist? Were you upset by some of the things I said to you? The things we talked about here?

D1: At first I was very upset.

Z: Really? In what way?

D1: Well, I disliked you.

Z: You disliked me? (laughter)

M: How can you say that without knowing him?

D1: Well, it wasn't really you I disliked. I disliked the things that you were saying.

Commentary

Z: I think some issues that arise in the follow-up segment are worthwhile making a few comments on. I was naturally pleased at the practical steps taken by the girls to enter the program at the vocational center. Naturally one can't tell whether that program will be completed; or what the durability of that change is. But I was pleased to see that initiative shown by the girls: their return to some type of activity that other girls of their ages are doing.

What is the problem with the family? Well, certainly one can see it from an individual point of view as a display of various types of symptoms in the girls individually. As a family therapist, I saw it as a generational problem and also to some extent as a cultural problem. There is the dispersion of authority from the parents to the daughters. Culturally, I would see it as a pattern of idealism and intellectuality in a Jewish family of this particular economic level.

I chose not to apply any labels to the problems; certainly not any psychiatric ones. I worked with them as a therapist who personally was dissatisfied with what they were doing with themselves, and as one who wanted more for them. If they didn't want more for themselves, I wanted more for them and I said as much. Now there were two incidents or moments in the latter session which caught my attention. In one the daughter says that she no longer has to please her father so much. She can live for herself a little bit more. I thought that this was a good statement from her. The girls and their father had been in a kind of coalition against mother, and I think to some extent that had been self-defeating. We see this a little bit more in the first session than in the follow-up, and it's one of the kinds of pathogenic relating in the family.

Another statement which pleased me was the mother's. The mother pops up with something like, "Well I've decided to live in spite of him," which I like because I'm for living instead of not living, and I

Z: think this expresses a sense of liberation in the mother which moved her from being less alive.

All say there has been change but no change; now that's paradoxical, isn't it? Change but no change. The younger daughter says that there has been change but it occurred only while the family was being seen in therapy. Then there was less depression and more togetherness as a group. The mother says that was also true: something was happening while the family was coming in, but things have returned to the old state, she says. The father kind of says that too, although he says something a little different: that they have learned something, implying that learning has carried over beyond the treatment series itself.

But they also talk about no change; about some kind of condition in the family which is very resistant to change. Perhaps this is more clearly stated by the 18 year old daughter, who is in a way the most isolated, the most negativistic in the family. She says there is no change. And yet she dresses differently and she's doing different things.

Change is a two-way process. For families to change, it depends greatly on how the *therapist* changes in the course of treatment. How does the therapist change here? Well, the therapist changes by coming to some kind of conclusion that what is wrong with the family is not psychiatric wrongness or a psychiatric problem. You notice that the therapist moves away from treating the family as if there were some kind of clearcut psychiatric problem. I think that it's an important decision for the therapist to make and to communicate. I think it has an impact on the family, which is very resistive to the judgments the therapist makes about it, and struggles with the therapist about the diagnostic judgments and about the procedures or prescriptions that the therapist might make up.

I think out of a collision of viewpoints between therapist and the family, something called change arises. It isn't a simple one-way street in which the therapist prescribes and the family responds. I don't know of any family to do that. I don't think of change in that fashion. I hope for a resistiveness on the part of the family to what I am trying to promote. In the 8th session I am to some extent acting a little "square," siding with the parents, but not so strictly that the girls don't perceive that there is a basis to try to move me away from the position of siding with the parents.

If there is a principle of family therapy that needs stressing, it is that change is an outcome of negotiation between the therapist and the members of the family. By negotiation I mean that the therapist may present his ideas about change to the family and he may pursue

Z: those, but he must understand that they will not be accepted totally. Characteristically the family will make efforts to get a change in his formulation. As they make these efforts to get the *therapist* to change his formulation, in the process *they* change. It isn't simply a matter of passing down a prescription for change.

    Some families are much readier for change than others, and I think one of the great tasks for the therapist is to try to make some assessment of that. It must be based certainly on many background features of families. Which ones are going to meet the therapist part of the way? In some instances the capacities for change are very limited, and I think it would be a foolish therapist whose expectations would be too high.

CHAPTER 2

RUNAWAY WIFE: PART I

The couple reported in this chapter and in Chapter 3 present a distressed marriage and family situation. A major symptom, although by no means the only one, was the wife's tendency to run away when under stress. She had left her husband and children on several occasions.

The interview presented here, the fifth interview with the couple, was recorded on videotape in March, 1972. I asked two co-workers, Dr. Philip Friedman, a psychologist, and Mrs. Margaret Olson (Roache), a psychiatric nurse, to observe the interview directly and discuss it with me afterward.

In the interview the wife's comments are designated by the letter W; the husband's, by H. Mine are designated by Z. Dr. Friedman's comments during the discussion that follows the interview are designated by the letter F; Mrs. Olson's, by O.

Introductory Comments

Z: Good morning, ladies and gentlemen. This morning we'll hold an interview with a couple, a young couple. Prior to that interview, which will start in a couple of minutes, I want to describe the couple to you very briefly. We will then have the interview. Following it I'd like to share a few thoughts with you about that interview—about some of the impressions the couple made on me, with a few words about the method or technique of working with them. Following that I would like to invite two colleagues who are here in the studio to share with me some of their thoughts.

This is a couple in their early thirties. They have four children; four daughters, ages 4 to 9. I must point out that the first session was one in which the wife was not present. The husband appeared with the four daughters. He told me he had been referred by his family doctor because of depression. This was not the first but the third time his wife had left the family.

The husband, indeed, was depressed. The children, I would say, were also depressed. I told him at the time of the first meeting that I couldn't quite see what we could do in family treatment. I thought it might be possible for him to receive some sort of needed direction individually or for the children individually, if it were indicated. But it didn't appear

Z: to me too promising a prospect for family therapy because there wasn't a wife present. I did ask the husband to come in again, I think mainly because I was concerned about his mental status—the depth of the depression.

He did not return for his second appointment and I lost contact with him for several weeks. Then about 5 weeks later I received a phone call. He said that he had been in contact with his wife and that he had gotten her approval to come in for an interview. So I asked that he come in with her to assess the situation.

This is a white couple. The husband is a mechanic in a meat-packing plant. They reside in Northeast Philadelphia, but have their origins in the old Kensington neighborhood. This is a Protestant couple, although there's been some changing of denomination over to the husband's, which I believe is Episcopal.

Let me see if there are other basic facts that will be helpful in orienting you. This will be the 5th or 6th interview, depending on whether you count that first one with the husband and children alone as an interview. Their recent appointments have been kept regularly. At first they were weekly; currently they are bi-weekly. The level of education of the couple would be into high school, although I don't recall if either completed high school. Now I think that gives you some basic information about this couple and I will now get them and we will conduct our interview.

Fifth Interview (March, 1972)

Z: I told you last week that videotaping this type of procedure makes it more difficult. It's difficult on all of us. I think it adds a special stress, so I want to remind you, as I did last week, when I talked to you about this meeting, that the purpose is training, which is what we do here; and also that there may be things that you do not feel comfortable talking about in the presence of the cameras, and that's all right with me. All you have to do is signal, raise a little finger or something; because I would perfectly agree with that point of view. Now insofar as we can, let's hear what's been going on with you.

W: Want to start with last night?

Z: (directed at wife) I turned to you because you're the talker in the family. I can't hardly get anything out of you. (at husband)

W: We had a good blow-out last night.

Z: Yeah?

W: Yeah, we had a—fisticuffs, you could say. In other words he got—

Z: Does it show? Are there marks?

W: Yeah!

Z: Where?

W: All over my body. (laughs) On my back and all; my hands.

Z: How did that happen?

W: I don't know. I turned around—We had been out during the day. He had to go to the dentist and the dentist was closed.

H: Yeah.

W: And then we came back from there and I said I was going to make supper for the kids, and for some odd reason he blew his top and he just went berserk. And after he went berserk he came after me and started beating me up.

Z: This was last night?

W: Yes, this was yesterday.

Z: What time was it?

W: About five o'clock.

Z: And you were preparing—

W: I was going out. I didn't even get started. I was going out to make it.

Z: And you were going out to make the dinner.

W: Uhuh.

Z: You were going out to buy something?

W: No, just out to the kitchen.

Z: Oh, the kitchen. And then all of a sudden, Rich went berserk.

W: Yeah, he went bananas on me for some reason.

Z: What happened? What happened?

H: I don't know; I just blew up.

W: He started telling me the baby wasn't his and this, that and the other; and he was going on a long string and—

Z: Oh, I see; I see, I see.

H: Well, earlier we had went down to where she used to be. She wanted to go down, and I said I didn't want to.

Z: Down where?

H: Down to the other neighborhood.

Z: She wanted to go down?

H: Yes.

Z: Oh; oh.

H: And I didn't want to go down and we went down. I said I'll go but I don't think we should. I said, eventually you're going to see them people.

Z: Them people, meaning—

H: Oh, the people she knows down there.

Z: Yeah, the people she knows down there.

W: I think we ran into about three of them—that's about all.

Z: What did you want to go down there for?

W: It was no real purpose in it. It's just that different things have been said and I said, maybe if we went down and we ran into this person it would clear a lot of the air of doubt that he might have in his mind as far as me wanting to go back there again.

Z: These are things that Rich has said?

W: Yeah.

Z: Things that Rich has said.

W: Yes, and when I said that to him he said, well I guess you're going to have to run into them eventually. He said, you might as well do it now and get it over with.

Z: Yeah.

W: And I figured this was a good way of clearing the air and getting it out of the way, and it's done and over with. Because in the beginning, when I first came home—

Z: That's what you thought. That's what you thought.

W: Yes. In the beginning when I first came home, Eddie (referring to the man she had been living with) had called a couple of places. He had called my mom's and he had called my sister-in-law's trying to find out where I was, and so forth. And then all of a sudden it stopped and there was no more to do about it. But I also told Richie. I said, I'm a little leery because of the type of person that he is. He's liable to come up to the neighborhood, watching him to see what time Richie goes to work and so forth—and maybe causing some kind of a problem when Richie's not around. I feel I could handle this myself—You know, if he should ever come up to the house—just call the cops and him being more or less picked up and taken away.

Z: Let's go back to the incident—although I'm sure this is connected with it, I'm sure it's connected with it. You were talking, Rich, when we got off the track.

H: Yeah. I guess I'm just brooding about it. I guess everything just caught up to me, I guess.

Z: You're jealous.

W: Extremely jealous.

Z: Extremely. I'd—I would be jealous.

W: I don't know why. To me, I'm nothing to be jealous about. I mean, it's not that I'm not trying at home, because I am.

H: Oh you are; you are.

W: I'm there constantly.

Z: What do you mean?

H: Trying.

Z: She is trying? Doing things around?

H: Doing things around the house.

Z: Keeping things straight.

H: Straight. The kids like to see her. They're glad she's back. I'm glad she's back.

W: Well, I must have made some type of impression because he was telling me to leave the house again last night.

Z: Now, go ahead—

W: When he was telling me to leave the house. In other words, he was telling me to leave—to get out of the house.

Z: (directed to husband) Yeah, but I want to know when, uh, when you whacked her or whatever you did. What did you do?

H: Oh, I don't know. I, uh, called her names and—

W: And literally pulled my hair out.

H: I pulled her hair. And—I couldn't tell you everything. I don't remember.

Z: You were a little upset, huh?

H: Yeah, I feel bad about it. I felt bad about it last night.

Z: And this was about—

H: I'm sorry it happened. I don't want it to happen.

Z: What did you say?

H: I said—I'm sorry, I had teeth out last night. I'm sorry it happened. I didn't want that to happen.

Z: When did you have your teeth out?

H: Last night.

W: I took him up to the dentist after everything calmed down.

H: About 9 o'clock.

Z: You mean after this?

H: Yeah.

Z: You went up to the dentist and then you had the work done? My God.

W: He has an advantage over me, for one thing. He's a man and I can't fight like a man. (laughs)

H: She swings good, though.

Z: Did you swing at him?

W: Yes, I did—in self-defense. I had to. I said, if I had had a frying pan in my hand I would have hit him with that too. You know, it's funny—I guess I'm just tired.

Z: Well, it sounds like you two must love each other a little bit in order to get that angry at each other. My goodness, it must mean something like that. In addition to other things, of course. But, uh—So there was some, uh, pushing around and swearing and so on. And you feel bad about it today.

H: I guess I—

Z: (to wife) Did you set that up? By that business of going over and visiting?

W: No!

Z: You don't think you did?

W: No, you could say—It wasn't that I really set it up; it's not that I planned it in advance.

Z: Did you ask Rich to take you over there?

W: I asked him if he wanted to go down and he said, yes. He figured that you were going to have to face them sooner or later and you might as well get it done and over with. And I figured by doing this, it would clear up any thoughts he had in his mind as far as me ever wanting to go back again.

Z: It sounded all very sensible, but—

W: Apparently it didn't work out that way.

Z: Apparently something else happened. When you went over—What did you do, drive over?

H: Yeah, we drove down.

Z: How far away is it?

H: It's about five or six blocks.

Z: Five or six blocks? Well, you could walk over there.

W: No, it's ten blocks.

Z: What happened when you drove over? Was it yesterday or the day before yesterday?

W: Yesterday.

Z: So it was in the morning? Or the afternoon?

H: In the afternoon.

Z: Yes. So this thing sort of mushroomed and snowballed.

W: Between leaving the other neighborhood where we were and coming back home again.

Z: Uhuh.

W: Everything seemed fine during the whole thing. I mean he was talking to people that I knew. He knew some of the people himself by being in the neighborhood at one time, and, uh, after we got home was when he exploded.

H: I don't know why I exploded. She said something—

Z: You knew why you exploded. You were angry and you were jealous, because I would feel the same way. So why did you say you didn't know why you exploded?

H: I mean just quick, like that.

Z: Yeah.

H: I mean I didn't feel funny or anything while we were down there.

Z: Did you know how angry you would get?

H: Well, I didn't think I would get that angry!

Z: Did you know that he would get that angry when you went down there?

W: Not at the time. But I've known his anger from before, when he was as mad as he was yesterday.

Z: He has been in the past—that mad?

W: Yes.

Z: So you've had these little episodes before? This is not the first time.

W: No, this is not the first time. This is the first time since I've been home. But previous times, like when we were married and all—I can remember one incident where he broke two of my ribs and never even knew it. I didn't know it until a few months later, and they had healed themselves and the nerve endings had rubbed together.

Z: Uhuh.

W: But I've had violent arguments with him before.

H: Like you say—

W: But I thought he'd calmed down some. But he's still as violent as that.

H: Like when we leave here, when we come visit, she doesn't say anything. Don't want to talk about it. She doesn't say that she doesn't want to talk. She gives me the impression that she doesn't want to talk about it.

Z: Oh, is that so; is that so?

H: She may say a few words and that's all; it's dropped.

Z: Yeah. Do you want to keep talking about the meeting?

H: No. Well, the points what we brought out and—

Z: But she doesn't want to talk?

H: Not all the time.

Z: Why do you think it's so?

H: I don't know. Sometimes she seems closed-mouthed.

Z: Is this true? You don't want to talk about it?

W: Yeah, when I leave I'm usually pretty quiet.

Z: A little depressed or something?

W: I guess; partially.

Z: Because why?

W: I really don't know why.

Z: When you leave, what about you? Are you depressed?

H: No.

W: He generally feels good.

H: I feel good because of things that are brought out. Like I said, she don't want to talk about some things, or some things I don't want to hear about. At least here she brings them out.

W: That's one other point. I don't feel very proud of myself either.

H: Well, some things have to be forgotten about.

Z: So what do these meetings—The kind of meeting this is, is a meeting in which she can say things she would not say at home.

H: It helps.

W: No, I say things at home. I refer to the general things. Yeah, I try to discuss things with you at home.

H: Yeah, some things you do.

W: But like, a lot of times he gets very perturbed at the fact that I don't talk much at home.

Z: Maybe you need me to help her talk better.

W: I can't very well talk at home. If his mother isn't dropping in, it's one of the kids; and I have to take care of them.

Z: Yeah.

W: And to me they come before anything else.

Z: You are living with—

W: His mother.

Z: Your mother-in-law.

W: Uhuh.

Z: And she pops in a lot I guess, does she?

W: Well, she pops in and out. It seems like every time she's popping in—

Z: It's her home; it's her home.

W: Yes. She's always involved in a conversation.

Z: With her—

W: But I've been very fidgety lately and he knows this, with my nerves and all. And I just can't sit in one place for longer than about an hour, because by the time I get done with the kids—I sit with them through breakfast. I sit with them through every meal that they have. But then he comes down and he wants to talk about a lot of things, and we can't really do any of this stuff right now. We have to wait until later when we have our house. I mean you can't plan too far in advance.

Z: Who interrupts you? Your children?

W: Them for one; my mother-in-law for another one.

Z: Who else?

W: That's it. Or if the phone rings or something like that. Or if someone was to call on the phone.

Z: So this is a place where your mother-in-law is not present here, at least not yet. And the kids are not here because I asked them not to be here. The phone is not going to ring. Does that help you two talk?

H: Uhuh.

W: Yeah. But what we discuss here isn't what he wants to discuss at home. It may sound dumb, but to me he goes on a long, long, unreasonably long way of getting one point across which *could* take five or ten minutes of my time. So I just don't think it's necessary. He explains so many things. He's like his mother. His mother could tell me something like ten years ago and she'll tell me the same thing like six months

W: from then. And I could tell her the stories of the family as good as she could tell them, because she has told them so many times. And he's the same way.

Z: Is that true?

H: That's the way mom is, but I didn't know I was like that.

W: He's the same way. He gets on a subject and he harps on it and he harps on it and harps on it.

Z: You didn't think you were the same way?

H: No.

W: But you are. (laughs)

Z: Have you told him that in the past?

W: Yeah. I said, do you have to drag it out so long?

H: Well, I don't think I was dragging it out.

W: He gets on my nerves, (laughs) and then that's when I lose all my patience. And I just can't sit there and discuss it.

Z: When you lose your patience, what do you do? Do you take off?

W: I just say, I got to go do the wash or I gotta do this or I gotta go do that or something else. I have to in order to just try to stop him and make him realize that: Richie, we already discussed this for the past three hours and we haven't gotten anywheres.

Z: You can't get him to respond to you the way you want him to, so you—

W: No. And then he complains about the same thing; that he can't get me to respond to his way.

Z: So you run off.

W: But like I said, it takes him a hour.

Z: What do you want from her? What do you want from her though? She said you best stop telling those long stories. (wife laughs) But what is it you want from her?

H: Well, I guess maybe it's because she doesn't say much. She don't give you a definite answer. Like coming over here, she just opened up and started talking about a house. Her sister has a nice house, and we went up there the other day—

W: This is my other sister.

Z: So you're looking for a house? Are you seriously looking for a house?

H: Yeah. Well we're not out looking; we're trying to get an idea.

W: An idea of what we want. Because we figure what we have we're going to be spending quite a lot of time in it. You know, a lot of years.

Z: But you had your eye on something, didn't you?

H: Yeah.

W: Oh, yeah. My one sister's house, but, uh—

Z: But that isn't suitable?

W: Since then I've seen my other sister's house again and I sort of like the idea that she has. 'Cause it's a ranch-type home; it's all on one level.

Z: Where does she live?

W: She lives in Cornwell Heights.

Z: It's more out?

W: Yeah, it's further out and the yard is bigger. And I keep thinking we have one on the way and two of them are still fairly small.

Z: Is that for certain now?

W: Oh, yeah. I went to the doctor's and found that out and had a pregnancy test. It all came out positive.

Z: When did you find that out for sure?

W: Friday I went to the doctor's and Monday for sure.

Z: Friday you went to the doctor and Monday he called, or what?

W: Monday I called him and found out my tests had come back positive.

Z: So Monday you found out you were pregnant, and Tuesday was the big battle, and Wednesday you are here. Quite a week already. You can settle down for the rest of the week; it's all right with me. (wife laughs)

H: It's all right with me if we settle down for the rest of the year!

Z: No, I think you have too much trouble between you, and too many things to work out.

H: Well, Sunday night I worked 11 to 7. I worked Sunday night and I stayed and worked 7 to 3. I did a turn-around; went home for 8 and went back and did another 8.

Z: Sunday?

H: Monday night. Sunday night 11 to 7, and stayed Monday 7 to 3. That was Monday afternoon I went home and I went back in Monday night, 11 to 7.

Z: Was that because you wanted to do that or because—

W: That was so we could make arrangements for coming in here.

H: See, we had a fellow get hurt in work; so that changed my schedule.

Z: In order to get here this morning?

H: So they changed my schedule and I had to go back in Monday night.

Z: So, added to everything was that you were kind of tired.

H: I think so.

Z: Yeah.

H: And I don't like dentists.

W: Yeah. And I think he had that preying on his mind too, the dentist. He doesn't particularly like to go.

H: We went up yesterday morning and he wasn't there. He had—

Z: Is this something you've been putting off?

H: Yeah, really. But I just wanted to go and get it done because they were hurting me bad. When I had the accident all the teeth were cracked and shattered. When I had the automobile accident.

Z: Yeah. Was that a couple of years ago?

H: Yeah, two years now. So they were starting to bother me and I thought I'd go get it over with. She got an impression for her—

W: Bottom teeth.

Z: Well, have you talked about the most important things now? It was the battle; the visit to wherever that is—

H: Well, I don't like to battle—

Z: The teeth; the double work shift. Is that mostly what has happened? Well, that's enough for a week!

H: I don't like to battle, but she told me again—How did she put it: she said, if you do that again I'm going to hit you with a frying pan, and—

W: And I meant it.

Z: Do what again?

H: Have another battle like that.

Z: If this happens again she's going to hit you with a frying pan?

H: With a frying pan, yeah. She said, I ain't going nowhere. At the end of it there was a lot in just a few words that meant a lot, even after the battle.

Z: After the battle last night you said, if you do it again I'm going to hit you with a frying pan.

W: I told him if he did it again I was going to hit him with a frying pan.

Z: But you also said you aren't going anywhere.

W: No, I have no intentions of walking out that door. I'm home; I feel safe and sound.

Z: So you knew what he was worried about.

W: I don't see why. He knows I've been home. He's here all the time. All he has to do is pick up the—

Z: What do you mean, you don't see why? Of course you see why!

W: Why? Why should he feel that way? He knows I'm home. He knows I'm in the house.

Z: Look, if I know what he's saying, you know what he's saying.

W: I think he's going by what you say because he'll say I could probably do it again. I know I could do it again.

Z: I didn't say you could do it again or not do it again. I'm saying that he knows you've been away three times, right, three times. So this is in his mind; you know it's in his mind. He's fearful about it. You know he's concerned about it. So you knew what he was saying to you, and you gave him some reassurance on that score; and you knew how important it was to him.

W: But I tell him this every day.

Z: He needed to be reassured that you are not going to take off again. He's entitled to that. (wife cries) What are you crying about? What's she crying about?

H: I don't know.

Z: You don't know? You have no idea? Does she feel bad? She must feel bad.

H: She feels bad. I feel bad.

Z: But you feel bad because of what you did last night, right?

H: Yeah.

Z: You didn't like to blow up like that. You didn't like to hit her.

H: No.

Z: And she feels bad because she, uh, she feels guilty; she feels she has let people down, is that right? Or why?

W: No. It's just the opposite way around.

Z: What is the opposite, then?

W: Maybe I'm trying too hard to prove my point.

H: She made me realize that last night. She said that even after the battle and it was good.

Z: You felt good about it?

H: I felt good about it even with the battle and everything. She came out and she said that. Even made me feel worser.

Z: Well maybe it was worth having then, I don't know. We will see.

W: (tearful) I don't like to fight. I went through two years of having the shit beat out of me day in and day out. I think I've been kicked around enough. I don't need to be kicked around by my husband. If he wants a dog to kick around, then let him get a dog to kick around, not me.

Z: What's the two years you're talking about?

W: When I was living with Eddie.

Z: Yeah.

W: He knows. He's seen the marks all over me. Last night was like a nightmare; just like being down on Kensington Avenue again going through the same thing.

H: I don't want her to feel like that; but after last night she can't help feeling like that.

W: Now it only created another worry. I don't know whether I'll lose the baby while carrying it; or whether something will happen to it when it's born. Now I got that to worry about for the next seven months. And yesterday I wished I would have lost it if it's going to create so many problems. The kids turned around to him last night and said, if you're going to throw Mommy out then we're going with her, and all of them wanted to do the same thing.

Z: They were on her side.

H: They were on her side.

W: They were on my side.

Z: Well, of course you see it as a bad thing because you took—you were on the receiving end yesterday mostly, I guess.

W: Well the kids saw it too, which didn't help them either.

Z: Well, they lined up with you, you know, which is probably a change. They lined up with you, and I'm still not so sure it's bad that it happened. I don't like to see you beat up, don't get me wrong. I'm not saying that I like that. It's not good; but at this time, I don't know how you can avoid episodes in which something like that might happen. I'm not encouraging them, I'm really not, I don't like them; but under the circumstances it may not have been such a bad thing. That's as an outsider. I wasn't there; I didn't have to take the—

W: Yeah.

Z: The abuse. So you see, in a way it might be easier for me to say that to you. It may sound that way. But it was one of those days that tensions were growing higher and higher. And you contributed to that.

Z: You weren't a helpless little lamb; you contributed to that. So I don't want to push it all on his shoulders.

W: Oh, no, I'm not saying that it's all his fault.

Z: Because I don't think it was all his fault. I think you contributed to it. So, uh, you must share in some of it. If you want to call it blame, all right call it blame or guilt or whatever. Some of you needed that, uh, attack or whatever was involved there. Well this has been a very interesting meeting today; and surprisingly because, you know, it's not like a regular meeting where we'd be off by ourselves. I want to thank you for making it an interesting meeting, and a meeting I think you'll get something out of in spite of, you know, the circumstances. Because, uh, you have a lot on your minds. It was good that you could bring that out as you have. I like you to use the meetings that way because I don't think you have enough time outside here; and also you need me because, uh, you need somebody to referee, right?

W: Yeah. You take when you have two mothers-in-law: one mother is likely to take one part and see one part, and the other mother's likely to see the other part; and that's not really a referee.

Z: No, no, that's not a referee. I'm the referee because I'm still kind of a stranger to you, right? So I don't have to be more loyal to one or the other, or more involved with one or the other. I can blame you both equally.

W: (laughs) Yeah, I know.

Commentary and Discussion

Z: At times the therapist is a celebrant of major events in family life and acts something like a priest or civic official who confirms that an event has occurred; or that a relationship that once existed has been broken; or that a relationship has been restored. Of course, the celebrant is in a powerful position and it can be a therapeutic position to help seal a desirable change or influence the direction of change. In the case of this couple, the therapist is a celebrant of their coming together again to live as man and wife.

Having experienced much bitterness and hardship in their marriage, the couple must explore their potentiality at this time to live in some harmony. The therapist must try to introduce new directions, new attitudes, new options; and to deal with the predictable efforts of the couple, in their doubt and indecision, to minimize his interventions. Thus although he starts out as a celebrant of the change which has

Z: already occurred and which may be desirable, eventually the therapist must shift from that role and act as a skillful negotiator with the couple as they face their hard day to day struggles.

It's very early in the work with this couple. I want to highlight a couple of things and also try to put it tentatively in a context. I want to recall to you that it is a situation in which a change had occurred between the first meeting and the second. Between the first and second, the wife returned to the home. Between the first and second, the context of the therapy also changed because present in the first meeting were the husband and the children. In the second I asked that the children not participate. Just the husband and the wife participated and they have done so religiously, I must say.

At this time they seem to need the therapy and/or the therapist, as I think you see. They are engaged; it's not a question of engaging this family as with so many families, particularly the lower economic classes. They are engaged in the treatment; they are taking from the treatment; they are giving to the treatment. They're taking from me, the therapist; and they're giving to me, the therapist. I like them both as people. They have their interests and these interests are not the same. From the standpoint of the wife, she is interested in demonstrating to her husband that she is serious about her intention to remain at home. He has his own interest, and that is to find some outside authority that will help reinforce his position as a husband to her; who will strengthen that position, that authority, and convince her that she should remain with him and with the children, and so on. This man was deeply depressed at the first meeting; he was drinking heavily. There has been a history of rather heavy drinking on both sides here. And he is no longer so depressed, although I think we see him in some kind of mood because of what occurred. And he is not drinking heavily. So symptomatically, at that level, we see considerable improvement.

Now here we have these mutual interests of husband and wife in the therapy. What are the interests of the therapist? I don't think they can be identical to those of either the wife or the husband. As I mentioned to the wife at some point late in the interview, I'm not a mother-in-law or your mother; so I'm not on his side or I'm not on your side—I'm outside. We see the need of the therapist to establish himself as an outsider *and* an insider; as somebody who has his own interests and can take positions independently of both husband and wife. He can introduce something new because they do need something new introduced into their lives. It is not going to be quite as she wants or as he wants, nor I'm afraid will it be quite as I want for them. But some-

Z: thing new, I hope, arises out of this chemical mixture that we do here in treatment sessions.

It's not simply a question of the wife's returning home in this case and the husband being satisfied and less depressed, and that's what our goal will be. That is not my goal as therapist. I would like something to happen between these two people that neither can predict for themselves and that has happened because I have been present in these sessions. And I think we have a good chance with them to do that.

Now I would like to ask Dr. Philip Friedman and Mrs. Margaret Olson to join me here, and to share some of their thoughts about viewing this family. Phil and Margaret have sat in the studio here. Who wants to start?

F: Well I had a couple of impressions, quite a few of which you summarized in the description you just made of the family. I was particularly interested in how you conducted the session, what your role was; and I had a number of observations some of which reinforce what you said. First of all, I was kind of impressed with the soothing quality of your voice alone through the session. There was, surprisingly under the circumstances, some rather personal material of a high emotional nature. I don't know if this is your general style, but it was a soft soothing quality to your voice which definitely had an effect on the couple.

You have emphasized in your writing the side-taking function of the family therapist, and I think today—and I'm sure in other sessions it may differ—but today you tended to rather consistently side with the husband. I thought you made numerous points about, maybe she set it up, and man to man, you said, I would feel jealous and angry also— which I thought was a good point. You chose to side with him on numerous occasions today, which he no doubt needed, and in a sense I think to encourage her to reassure him.

I was also interested in how you handled the situation of the battle between them, indicating that there was some very positive effect of that battle. Despite talking about all the bruises, she said it was a good battle—that was her opening word—a good battle! She may have felt some guilt about provoking the battle, but your comment later also was that there may have been some good things that occurred from that.

But I wasn't sure whether perhaps you weren't giving them two messages. You said, I really don't like that you fight, but perhaps you were showing by being angry that you loved each other. In a way you were re-labelling for them the fight. But then you said, maybe it had

F: to occur. I thought perhaps that was your way of saying that some time in the future—it was kind of a double-bind, you see—continue this, but on a covert level stop at some time in the future under your own control. I thought that was the message you were giving. I'm not sure that was your intention, but that's how I perceived it. I'll stop for now.

Z: Yeah. I quite agree with what you've been saying. You know, there are some therapists who very much promote the idea of fighting, but I don't promote fighting. But as a realist once it occurs, you know, it's kind of foolish to say that it didn't occur. On the other hand, I think it's probably wise for the therapist to say, now that's not nice, you know, like a kind of a father or a mother. I think that's more or less a sound position. On the other hand, I'm a great believer in, you know, simply saying that what occurred did occur, and offer some comment on whether I approve or disapprove, more or less strong.

Now that's what I was doing. I was trying to make comments on the fact that it occurred and that there were good elements evolving from the battle and there were probably some undesirable elements evolving from the battle. Yeah, that's it. I don't think I stimulated the battle.

But here it happened, it erupted, and what I tried to do was simply to trace some of its antecedents, you know, what went into it. At least trace some of its elements that raised the level of tension to the point at which somebody was going to blow. And to establish her role in it, too.

F: I was interested too how carefully you went over that sequence, since I think many other family therapists would handle that very differently. Certainly many of them would not go through it detail by detail looking at the tension points that led up to it and siding kind of judiciously with the husband's conception of it. That I think probably characterizes your style.

Z: Not the style so much as it reflects a position or conceptual thing. I do want to know about those tension points in some detail. Maybe we'll get back to that.

O: I was interested too in how you handled that fight sequence. You looked at the immediate things that led up to the fight and I was thinking to myself, what would happen if the therapist would begin to pick up her feeling of humiliation and delved deeply into that feeling, and what it meant to her to be hurt and to be hit, and maybe even got into some historical meaning. That would have been even another way of

O: getting into that, and I wonder what the outcome of that way of handling it would have been.

Z: That's good because my immediate response is, she gave us a good example of having worked that herself when she burst into tears and said, I went through two years of that! Which was of course a recollection of her experience with another man. Two years of being kind of beaten around. Now of course, her own contributions to that whole process were conveniently forgotten in the emotion of the moment. She was crying and feeling regret and sorrow and was bitter. But she did that work herself. I didn't push her in a direct way about it. And he also was able to talk about how he felt badly following the battle, and now he even feels worse today, and so on.

But you're right, characteristically I don't follow up in a very direct way to get the more historical sequences, the sequences going back months or years. No, I don't do that because I don't think people recall very well anyhow, and when they recall they may recall things that didn't happen or probably didn't happen. So I like better this spontaneous comment when she says—Now to be sure, that was a recollection and yet it had some—She was playing a little game here. Now of course we were all involved in what she was doing. She was reacting in a very human way, and a very sincere way, recalling what she went through, the bitter times, in another experience. And yet at another level she, of course, was manipulating us both to kind of draw us into a fundamentally sympathetic position with respect to her. Now her husband feels bad enough as it is, so I didn't want to overdo that. So I said to her, now of course you're right but you know you played a little role in this yourself. In a sense, yes, she deserves support; but also she deserves a reminder that she has made contributions to this mess. And she gets something out of it; she gets a certain kind of kick out of it. This is not bad or it's not good. It's simply that she's a person and she has both negative and positive impulses, and we have to comment on both sides.

F: Margaret talks about the humiliation. I sense a lot of guilt in her, but even more is how she uses the guilt against her husband.

Z: Yes; yes she does.

F: She brings out the baby. She says, maybe you've killed the baby or damaged the baby.

Z: I got the feeling that she got kind of drawn into it, and maybe the setting itself had a little bit to do with overdramatizing that. I think

Z: the whole context here probably had its effect at that moment because I think the context, the videotaping, did have an effect on us today, in a sense that it heightened the likelihood of getting this material. I would say that sometimes videotaping can inhibit and sometimes it can free, so that I think the latter was happening today.

O: I was wondering about that, Jerry, because I was interested to hear you say that you felt kind of warmly towards these two people. And between the two of them was such a tension, or it seemed to be anyway, such an emotional barrier, that even the laughter which she attempted to throw out there fell flat.

Z: When did she do that? I didn't—

O: She would giggle periodically about the fight. She would laugh periodically, and I was struck by that laughter because she would put it out there and it just fell.

Z: I'm glad you brought that out because I was not aware of it.

F: I sense a lot of positive feelings. I wouldn't say just underneath all of the tension but—

Z: Oh yeah.

F: Some of it may have been in response to guilt. But some of it was quite genuine.

Z: I was responding by saying, in spite of all of this fighting it must mean that you love each other in some way. And there wasn't any denial of that. But also we had here today a fairly good example of the way they try—This love has been used in a very destructive way, more or less, between the two of them; as it often can be used that way. They are destroying each other, to some extent, with love. Yeah, I think you have to love somebody to be quite that—or destructive in that way; or let's say to have a bond, to want to visit on that person all of the feelings of pain and jealousy or vengefulness, you know. You have to feel something about a person to want them to feel that way. And she set him up to feel pretty jealous today; well, uh, expressed today but over the last two days. He denied it of course because he didn't want her to know how jealous he felt. And I said, but you do feel jealous because I say you feel jealous and I would have felt the same way, you know. And there's nothing wrong with it! Which upset her probably because she would have liked a lot of that not to be said.

F: Jealousy is one way of showing caring, I think.

Z: Yeah, it's one way of meaning you're involved. You know, you can't help being involved in what the other party does—that's jealousy. With all the deep bitter feeling that it can evoke. But she didn't want him to talk about his jealousy. She wanted him bottled up about it and she can shut the man up pretty well—by guilt, by all kinds of things. Now also she can shut him up by running away, which I'm sure she's done in the past.

CHAPTER 3

RUNAWAY WIFE: PART II

There were ten interviews with the couple presented in Chapter 2. Reported in this chapter is the ninth interview which was recorded on videotape in mid-May, 1972. Everything sounds rosy: there is good cooperation, affection, hope for the future. The interview was a brief one, lasting about half an hour.

There was one more interview held with the couple, but then appointments that were scheduled were not kept and contact with the couple was lost for about one year. In May, 1973, the husband telephoned to say that his wife had left him again. This time, however, she had taken her children with her and moved to her mother's home. The husband acknowledged that he had been abusive to his wife, but now he wanted her to return and hoped that if I agreed to see them again, it would persuade his wife to return.

In the transcript my comments are designated Z; the husband's, H; the wife's, W.

The Ninth Interview (May, 1972)

Z: What's been happening?

W: Oh, everything.

Z: Other than this—

W: Everything. The kids have gotten good report cards. We just came back. We took them away for the weekend, Saturday and Sunday.

Z: Where did you go?

W: To Lancaster County. To the Dutch Wonderland.

Z: Oh yeah, that's near Lancaster.

W: My daughter calls it Disneyland. From there we stayed in a motel overnight. They were fascinated by that.

Z: The kids? The four kids?

H/W: Yeah.

W: We had a great big room with three double beds in it. And from there on Sunday we drove up to Hershey—Hershey, Pa. And then from there we came down through Reading, Lebanon and—

H: The Stroudsburg railroad.

Z: The railroad? Take the kids on the railroad?

W: I'm worn out!

H: Yeah, well, we didn't ride the train.

W: They went on the President's car. They visited on that.

Z: When was this?

W: Just this past weekend.

Z: So you had a good time; it sounds like a good time.

H/W: Yeah, oh yeah.

W: I'm tired. (laughs) We walked all over.

Z: You were exhausted.

W: Yeah. We walked all over. Yes, we've had some pretty serious problems but we've managed to cure them ourselves.

Z: You've tried to handle them yourself?

W: Uhuh. And we seem to be doing pretty good by it. I just hit him in the head with the frying pan; there's no problem after that. (laughs)

Z: That sort of settles things down.

W: Keeps him quiet for a hour or two. (laughs)

H: I get some rest—I've been working like crazy.

Z: You mean with the job?

H: Yeah, 42 days straight.

Z: Forty-two days straight?

H: Two weeks of 12 hours on and 12 off.

W: With no time off. It was just a solid seven days a week. This is our first—We had a four-day weekend; it started Saturday.

H: Saturday, Sunday, Monday.

Z: Is that why you took it?

W: Well, we had planned it for about two and a half months with the kids about going up there and seeing these different things. They've all been looking forward to it and they've really been patient about it.

Z: Did you handle them all right? They didn't bug you too much?

W: No, only the ride on the amusements up there. But I mean that's only normal. But as far as them causing any problems, no; they've been great. They don't even worry too much about me being out of the house. If I'm out by myself for a little while now they don't worry about it; they know I'm coming back home.

Z: You know, I speculated when you didn't—The last time that I saw you—I think we had one meeting after that time that we videotaped.

H: Yeah.

Z: And, uh, I don't recall too much of that meeting, except that—

W: We had a big argument the day before.

Z: You were still—No longer going down to that place?

W: No.

Z: I know you had the big argument the day before the videotape. All right, yeah, then we went one week. The next week you came in and then we lost you. Was that due to anything in particular, or just one of those things?

W: No, it was just the way that he was working.

Z: It was your working schedule?

H: Yeah.

Z: Well, that's as good a reason as—

H: I've been working 12 hours on and 12 off. When I get done work I just come home and go to bed.

Z: That's your work schedule?

H: Twelve hours on. Working 12 and off 12.

Z: That's—

W: Besides his own eight hours he had four more to put in; and then there's only two of them working. So they had to work the 12 hour shift.

Z: 42 days straight?

W: No. That was two weeks straight of that.

H: That was two weeks of that. But the other was eight on and 16 off. One fellow got hurt; he got ammonia in his eye.

Z: Oh.

H: And he's hospitalized.

W: He's in the hospital.

H: Then my brother slipped and broke his foot.

W: And he was on—

H: That's when I was on vacation.

Z: Your brother and you work together?

H: He was out—

Z: And it was up to you?

H: Another guy and myself. Out of five of us it got down to two. That's why we were working like that.

Z: That's why you got on that kind of merry-go-round?

H: Yeah. And then when the other fellow came back off of vacation there was three guys to cover in 24 hours. But no relief man for weekends.

Z: OK. So it's just about two months since I've seen you.

W: Yeah.

H: The 21st.

Z: Was it the 21st? The last meeting, yeah, the 21st. You look good; you both look good; you—look—

W: Better. (laughter)

Z: You said it for me; you said it better.

W: You mean I don't look like that drab old hag? (laughs) That's what I felt like with this long brown hair. I felt like an oversized hippie walking around Philadelphia. (laughs)

H: You're looking good.

Z: You had ups and downs. Let's hear a little bit about those in the last couple months.

W: Go ahead. You started them all. (laughs)

H: I can't remember.

W: Well, they were really—They weren't serious, you know. Really they weren't battles or anything. Just like, minor disagreements. I couldn't even tell you what they were about, because I—

H: I can't remember.

Z: Nothing comes to mind?

W: No; they were that minor and that few, really.

H: I mean, there was nothing really serious.

W: No, there was nothing really serious about it. It's just that any problem we came across, we managed to more or less work it out. You know, to make sure that everything was all right without any big ado or argument or anything like that.

Z: No big blow-ups? After that one that you had; there hasn't been any?

H: No; even with all the working.

Z: Even with the pressure of working.

W: It's really been going along just beautifully.

Z: And the kids?

W: They've been fine.

Z: And your mother?

H: My mother? She's away now. No problem.

Z: Where's she at?

H: She's down at my brother's house in Jersey. Well, that's her other house. She's down there.

Z: Do you think she wants to be there?

H: Yeah.

W: Well, she goes back and forth and it's springtime and all of her flowers are out down there now, so she enjoys being down there.

Z: She takes care of them.

W: And she rummages through all of her junk and things that she saved over the years. She makes dolls and so forth. She's been trying to dig them out because my sister-in-law buried them and she can't find half of them, really.

Z: So the reason that you called me was that your schedule now—

H: Was broken, and we're getting back to normal.

Z: Back to normal.

H: Time off—

Z: So—Well, do we have anything to talk about? I don't know. Everything has been good for you?

W: Yeah, it has been.

Z: How have you been feeling now?

W: Let's see, I had the flu and I had a sinus infection on top of it; and then two days after that started, then I started having showings and we thought we were going to lose the baby. And on Saturday we were kind of upset by that because I had been so sick before with morning sickness, afternoon sickness and everything else. But now it's starting to pan out and I'm starting to feel a lot better.

Z: This would be about which month now?

W: I should be in my fourth month.

Z: The fourth?

W: Going into my fourth, yeah.

Z: Have you felt very much different than with any of the others?

W: Oh, have I!

Z: How?

W: Sick!

Z: You weren't sick before?

W: I was never sick with any of them. Never had a sick day in my life.

Z: This one, you felt—

W: With this one I've had morning sickness, afternoon sickness. I said, the only time I wasn't sick was when I was sleeping.

Z: What does your doctor say about it?

W: He says it's normal. But I'd like to know what normal is.

Z: Is he giving you much for it?

W: He gave me medication for it, but he told me when I first started and I was on nerve medicine from the doctor, he told me to stop taking the nerve medicine and he had given me a prescription. In case I did get sick, feel nauseated, then I could take the prescription; but like I said to Richie, I don't really need the nerve medicine any more.

H: She hasn't used that.

W: I found out that like over the period of time like since we were last here and everything else, my nerves aren't as bad as when I depended on the pills before. So that I'm more or less able to overcome most of the nervousness myself. And like being more adjusted now with the kids and the house and everything else you know, I'm able to cope with everything now. Like I said to him this morning coming down: I said, with the normal pace and the nice pace everything's been going between us, it doesn't take too much to really get upset. And it will seem like my stomach will just start churning if I do feel upset. Rich, do you have a hankie?

H: You have a cold?

W: Yeah, I still have a cold; I'm still coughing. My nose is clogged up. I just had it a couple of weeks ago.

Z: Sounds good.

W: No, it's not. It's the flu. (laughs)

Z: No, I'm not talking about—

W: I was flat on my back for four days. (laughs)

Z: You were out for four days?

W: Yeah, my mom came down because his mom is away.

Z: Is there anything I could be of—

H: No, no, we've been too busy.

W: No, I took the kids down, not this weekend but the weekend before. I took Richie down to work, and I took the kids and I went and picked up my mom and drove them all the way down to Atlantic City and

W: all the way back home again. And they had a ball that day because they ran all over the boardwalk. That was another time, another experience—walking all around. (laughs)

Z: The house, the house—you were looking for a house.

H: We've decided to wait.

Z: You've decided to wait? Until when?

H: Yeah, until we get more money.

Z: More money?

H: Where we're at now, it's easier for her. My mother will be there when she has the baby and then she'll have help; and she's going to have an operation afterwards.

W: I'm going to have an operation.

Z: Who is?

W: I am. I'm going to have my uterus removed afterwards because I have the Rh factor. The doctor said that since one was an Rh factor and this one will be one, he said five children is enough to have, and he said the only thing you're doing is endangering yourself and the baby more. We had talked about it before and then the doctor more or less confirmed it for us. For medical reasons. What else have we done?

H: We're going to stay there until she's back on her feet and then start looking. Because my mom will be there to give her a hand.

W: Well we have a bathroom right on the first floor, and when I come home, the only thing I'm supposed to be able to take care of is the baby; so this way it's just more convenient being on the first floor all day long.

Z: OK. Now, I can't think of a heck of a lot to ask, really. I'm delighted that you look the way that you do and that you sound the way you do, and that you look like you're liking each other, which is terrific. The way that you are each looking at each other opposed to the way you were looking at each other the last time, or certainly the first few meetings that I saw you. So I don't have a heck of a lot to ask you. The only thing—

W: Oh, I did do one thing. Shall I tell him about what I did that Monday? I went to the doctor's, well, it will be three weeks ago on a Monday.

H: Oh, yeah.

W: And I went to the doctor's in the afternoon. Richie was home; he was sleeping. And after the doctor's I had the notion to go down and go to my old neighborhood where I had been living; and I went down and I faced Eddie face to face and found out there was nothing there.

W: And I came back and I was very happy about it; and I woke Richie up and I told him I done it and there's nothing there. And I more or less gave myself an inner relief of any anxieties that might crop up in the future. I just put a stop to it right then and there. And I really felt good about it. And I explained how I felt about it to Richie and he understood. There was no argument from it or no misunderstanding or anything else. If you feel better, he said, then it was worth it.

Z: This was three weeks ago?

W: Yeah, this was three weeks ago.

Z: On Monday?

W: Uhuh, on Monday in the afternoon.

Z: So you went down—

W: Uhuh.

Z: And you talked with Eddie?

W: Uhuh.

Z: And you found out about—

W: Yeah, I came right home and told him.

Z: OK.

W: There's no lies between us. I feel as though anything I have to say, I can just tell Richie and it's understanding and all.

Z: All right, I'm glad to hear that too. Mainly the way it happened and what happened—Richie's response to it. It was a good response.

W: I think it was too. It made me feel as though anything I had to tell him—

Z: Yeah. It hasn't come up again?

W: No, there's been no repercussions from it or anything else, no.

Z: And you didn't hit each other with a frying pan?

H/W: No! (laughter)

Z: Now actually, the only thing that—There are two questions: one is, how often we should get together just for the sake of keeping in touch and hearing about you. But I'm not too convinced we need to meet weekly.

W: Do you think once a month?

H: We were going every two weeks.

Z: Oh, you started off once a week and then we switched to once every other week; and now the question is, should we keep it at the once

Z: every other week? Or should we just for a while make it on a once a month basis?

W: That's what I was thinking; maybe once a month.

H: Once a month.

W: Once a month basis because then there would be more to tell.

Z: I think maybe we can make it once a month for a while and see what things are like.

W: Now we have the two kids; they're going to go to camp. I think Ginger will be going to a day camp; she'll be going from nine to three. And then Elaine will be going away for a whole week with the Girl Scouts, and Nancy is with the Brownies.

Z: Well, let's make the next meeting in four Tuesdays. What's today, the 16th?

W: The 16th.

Z: Well, it would be in four Tuesdays at 10 a.m.

W: That will be fine because if his mom's not there, it would be more convenient.

Z: All right, that's settled. Now the next thing and the last thing for today, because I don't have much more to talk to you about unless you want—or there's something you want to—something else—

W: I don't know. Is there something I haven't covered?

H: No, everything's been going good.

Z: The other thing—

W: It has been, really. I'm really surprised myself. It's like I said, we've been able to communicate with each other on a lot more decent basis. Whereas we're not down one another's throat or anything like that. And if we do come across something, we try to kid around about it if it seems to get too hot and heavy in an argument. And we've been able to subside it and work our way out of it. Which I think is good. I think it's a great accomplishment.

Z: It is a big help, sure.

W: Because I can remember the last argument we had; we were both down each other's throat.

Z: That was the one—

W: Yeah, that was the battle, the Battle of the Bulge. (laughs)

Z: That was a big battle, all right.

W: I think I scared him out of it, that's why. (laughs)

Z: Now I don't like to rehash with you too much because, I think, you know, rehashing all the things sometimes is not too desirable. Maybe before we end today—What role do you think these kind of meetings have played? Have they played any role in what's happening between the two of you?

W: I think they have.

Z: You think they have?

W: 'Cause I find if I really find myself in a corner—If I can't get out of it myself, and even if I've talked to Richie and I don't think Richie can help me with it, I feel as though maybe I can find my answer here. At least I have that much hope; that I know if something does crop up and I don't think I can handle it, or Richie can handle it, that maybe you'll have an answer for it.

H: It's like you said once before—to referee.

W: There's another thing too. I said to Richie, I don't feel like I'm going in circles any more. I feel as though I found my purpose, and I feel as though I've reached the goal that I kept running to all the time; kept running away from. I feel as though I've found it. I could have stayed at home and found it, really.

Z: All right. Life isn't, you know, at an end for either of you. You have a long time to go and who knows what things will bring along. Sometimes they bring good things; often they bring bad things. So nobody is able to foresee those things. And there may be bad times again, but for now you have to live the days as they come along, and you found something with each other this time which maybe you hadn't found before. Looks like that may be.

W: I think I've grown up quite a bit.

H: Yeah, she has changed a lot.

Z: She has changed a lot? You see that?

H: I see that, yeah.

Z: Did you see it at first when she came back?

H: No, no; it's been a while. She's—

W: A ding-a-ling. (laughs)

Z: A what?

W: A ding-a-ling. (laughter)

H: Her outlook on things is different. She doesn't keep as much inside of her as she used to.

Z: She comes out more with things.

H: She comes out with things.

Z: So you don't feel locked out, like you used to.

H: I don't feel locked out and I understand her better.

Z: One of your complaints about him was that he talked too much.

W: Sometimes he does.

Z: He repeats.

W: Yeah, he gets on those lectures.

Z: Which is like his mother. (laughter) That's not so bad any more? You can tolerate that?

W: Well,—

Z: You don't—

W: No, he's been pretty good about it; I have to say that. Last night he started lecturing me, but that—(laughs)

Z: Now, you're agreed that—He was lecturing you last night?

W: Yeah, just a little bit; not too much.

Z: You're agreed that one of the uses of our meeting has been that you have needed a referee. Which I think is a good reason for the meetings. This has been the main reason? Would you say this is the main way it has helped?

H: I would say it's not her family, it's not my family—It's, you know—

W: It's an outsider.

H: It's an outsider. They might tend to favor my side over her side, and you don't get an honest opinion.

Z: When you came back I'm sure there must have been doubt and fear.

W: Yeah, there was fear I would find something wrong. And in fact when we had the fight that we had, I think it put a fear in both of us that I would pick up and leave again.

Z: Yeah, take off.

W: Which he says himself to me that if I did, he could understand why I did. But then the biggest challenge was to stick it out because it's not always like that. I think the main reason why it happened was because I caused it by going down to the other neighborhood; the both of us together, and—

Z: You caused it that time?

W: Uhuh. And I feel that Richard's been very understanding. I know he loves me and I love him.

Z: Yeah, I can recall mentioning this to you that day, that you caused—

W: Yeah, he was really afraid a couple of times that I wouldn't be there at night when he got home; that I would have taken off. But it's like I said to him and like I said to quite a few people, the main thing is just sticking it out, no matter how awful it seems. Because it's not just you, it's your children.

Z: It is rough.

W: It's your husband.

Z: It's rough; living together is rough, I don't care who it is. I don't care who it is.

W: Everybody has their ups and downs; you just have to go along with it, that's all.

Z: We try, we try; but it's not always possible. But it's rough for everybody. You know, that's one of the lessons of married life. You look around and you look at yourself, your own marriage; and you say, this is a hard thing to work out over a long period of time. When you came back this last time, why did you accept this idea?

W: There's been quite a few times that I've asked Richie before for psychiatric help.

Z: Yeah?

W: For my own benefit, not for him or the children; I've asked for it for myself. But Richie had said I never needed it. He said it was just something I should be able to work out by myself. And I guess I've just held that in the back of my mind. For the last two years I was realizing how I was wasting my time, and not being with my children. I mean that's where I should have been because I devoted all of that life to them before; and that's all I could think about when I was away from the children. Even though it didn't show outwardly it did inwardly; and I just said, it's got to be me.

Z: You're a pretty good mother, I think.

W: I try to be.

Z: You're a pretty good mother and you are certainly entitled to that role. Because you're good at it. Did you have any feeling about those first few meetings with your wife; any expectation about it? You yourself could have said: what do I need that for; she's back—that's fine.

H: No. I felt—Well, I came down first with the girls and saw her and—

W: And when you first put it to me, you made it sound like I was a real kook, (laughs) or what's another name for it.

H: I saw her and I gave her the address and everything as I was on my way to work. I just bumped into her and—

Z: That's what happened? You just happened to bump into her that morning or whenever it was?

H: Yeah.

W: That was before your first visit, when you brought the kids down with you.

H: Yeah, and I told you the address.

W: Yeah; and I said, you're the one that's nuts. You go tell them I don't need it. (laughs)

Z: So that's how it happened.

H: Yeah.

Z: That's how it happened. Sort of half coincidence.

W: I called him that Sunday or I had called my mom first and I said, get in touch with Richie and tell him to make an appointment to go down and see the psychiatrist.

Z: Called your mother—

W: Well she had his phone number.

Z: You agreed to the idea. So you got together. Well, that clarifies in my own mind how that happened.

W: Well, he came over to my girlfriend's and he got me and took me out for a ride. And then we had a few drinks and we sat there talking for a while, and he took me up to my mom's. I stayed there that night and he came up the following day to make the appointment and brought me up some clothes. And then we had gone down and we got the kids. We took them out for a while. The kids all said, what are you wearing to bed tonight, Mom; we got your nightgowns and all ready for you. So they just wanted me home right then and there. So I went right home. They're very persuasive, my children. (laughs)

Z: Well, yes, they were. That's a lot of persuasion.

W: They just wanted their mom home.

Z: Well, they still must like you.

W: Yeah, I think they do.

Z: That's kind of good. All right, let's call it quits for today and see you in four weeks. I was so glad to see you both this way.

Commentary (May, 1973)—A Follow-up on the Couple After One Year

Z: I want to bring things up to date on the couple. The ninth interview was done on May 15th, 1972. There was some thought that the couple and I

Z: would get together about a month later, simply to review what was happening with them. One can surmise from the interaction that there had been and might well continue to be a good deal of turmoil with this young couple. So many things had happened in their lives that I think it would be somewhat an idealization to hope that those would dissolve as a result of their experience with me or any other experience of a similar type.

I of course hoped, as I think every therapist hopes, that the impact of the work would be of a nature to carry through; that it would have duration in their lives beyond the months during which I was seeing them. Because it appeared to have a clear positive effect during that time and during the time from the first long interview which was videotaped until the follow-up of two months later. I more or less surmised that for a while things would continue in a fairly controlled or benign state. Now they did not come in for the interviews as I rather hoped they would. I'd hoped I would continue to see them on about a monthly basis—once a month. They did not pick that opportunity up. Many months passed and during those months from time to time as I would look at the record, I would remind myself of the couple, reconfirm my hopes for them, and hope that the absence of telephone calls was a good sign rather than a bad sign. I wondered whether the pregnancy had gone well, and whether the delivery had occurred, and if the baby was a girl or a boy, and so on.

About one year passed since the interview. Then in May, 1973, my secretary received a telephone call from the young husband. The telephone call informed her, I wasn't present at the time, that the couple had been separated for about one month. The wife left the home again. In a call returned to the young husband, we learned further that the wife had taken her children this time. Previous departures from the family had been by herself without the children; the children had remained with the husband and the husband's mother who was caretaker during those times. This was something new, and although I was quite disappointed with the recent episode, so far as I knew about it via the telephone call, I thought it was a shift or change of some kind from what had been occurring before in their lives. I looked forward to the possibility of seeing them both. The husband stated that he would like his wife to come in with him. She was not with him, living with him, but he hoped by telling her that he wanted to see me and have interviews, further interviews, that she would be persuaded to come. I agreed and I gave a time for the interview during the following week.

Z: On May 8th or 9th, 1973, I received a telephone call from the young wife. She told me that she wasn't willing to come in for the interview; that she had heard from her husband that he wished one. She refused that and very briefly told me of one or two circumstances that led to her separation.

In brief they were that shortly after seeing me in May of '72, her husband returned to heavier drinking, began brooding, and he raised questions about the paternity of the child, of the expected child. There was some physical abusiveness involved. She had her fill and after sticking for roughly nine or ten months, gathered the children up, said she was leaving and left, moving to her mother's home. She is currently living in her mother's home, taking care of the children who she said were happy and were in school. They seemed to accept the situation. She felt there was too much tension for the children while living with her husband; they were much too aware of his abusiveness.

In a telephone call the following day we talked more at length about the circumstances leading to the separation in April, 1973. More or less, I believed what she was telling me. I believed it and did not apply much pressure on her to be seen with her husband in a joint interview. I felt some concern for her well-being and felt that an interview might raise too many tensions at this time. I told her that I was very pleased that she had called and was so informative; that I wished her well and to keep in touch if she felt there was a need to talk further about anything. Incidentally, the pregnancy resulted in a birth during August of 1972. As a result of some complications, the infant died within 24 hours.

The following day was the day planned for the interview. I had some doubts whether the husband would come in. Of course I knew the wife would not be in, because we decided that on the previous day. I was hopeful of seeing the young husband, however, and asking him about the circumstances of the separation, as I did his wife. The interview was due at ten o'clock. He did not appear for it. However at 10:30 a.m. he telephoned. I took the telephone call and asked him if he intended to come in that day. He indicated no, that he had had some trouble at work. He asked me if I had been in touch with his wife. I said yes, but that she had declined to come in. He seemed not quite to know what to say, I think hopeful that somehow the knowledge that they would be coming to me would be enough to persuade his wife. I indicated nothing further about applying pressure to the wife; said nothing really about that except that I hoped that he would take advantage of the facilities or resources that were available to him. I said that it appeared that he and his wife could not get together at

Z: this time, but if he wished to come in for a brief meeting I would be happy to discuss with him alternative types of therapy or counseling that would be available to him. He didn't decline that although he didn't take it up immediately; he simply thanked me and said that he would consider it and perhaps call back. He seemed a bit tongue-tied on the telephone. I think he was hopeful that his wife had agreed to the interview. When he learned that she did not agree and that I did not pressure her to, I think he was just not ready for anything further.

Now these are the circumstances which I learned about one year later. Of course, one is disappointed. However as experienced professionals, we understand that so many things occur that we have relatively little control over. I simply want to remind you that this is the type of case one may see quite a number of. I think our capacities as therapists to work with such cases are limited, but that we should do just that; and that we have leverage in the situation.

I think the notion of the therapist as a celebrant of the couple is a legitimate notion, that it is a valid notion; but I want to remind you of what I believe also about the celebrant: that the role is available for a short time; it's very powerful for a short interval. It is interesting that after what they have both gone through, steps are taken to return to me. I would suggest that that is not coincidental. I like to think that the role I played with them a year or 15 months ago did indeed have a carry-over effect. Not of the kind that I would have hoped for most optimistically. But it did indeed have a carry-over effect. A year later the husband does telephone, and he's hopeful that by telephoning and engaging my cooperation, he can restore a situation with his wife, who at this time appears to have stabilized her situation in a way that I concluded was rather sensible. I thought her actions were rather mature, and I refused therefore to go along with the husband's interest. Indeed, however, he was hopeful of engaging me once again as a kind of celebrant. One sees couples like this frequently and one should not avoid working with them. The expectations should not be grandiose; they should be modest. A therapist comes to the family or is introduced to the family at a certain phase of its life. One is reminded of a flowing river or a flowing stream in which you kind of dip into the waters at one point; and it may be that you can influence the course of that river or stream by the act of dipping in.

CHAPTER 4

RUNAWAY WIFE: PROCEEDINGS OF A CASE CONFERENCE

The material that follows was first published in *Terapia Familiar*, the journal representing the Argentine Family Therapy Association. It is made available through the kindness of Alfredo Canevaro, editor-in-chief of *TF*, where it appeared in 1980 (Vol. 3, No. 5, pp. 140–164).

In April 1980 Dr. Canevaro organized a series of workshops and presentations for me in Argentina. He thought it would be stimulating if one of the presentations involved a small group of professionals exchanging views regarding a case of a couple I treated in 1972. I had made a film of the couple, and an analysis of the case plus full transcript of two interviews was later published in *Process and Practice in Family Therapy* (first edition).

I recall the event very well—a sunny, pleasant day, April 26, 1980, in Buenos Aires. My co-discussants were leading Argentine mental health professionals, including two psychiatrists, Dr. Jorge Garcia Badaracco and Alejandro Sicardi, and a psychologist, Licenciada Celia Elzufan. Dr. Canevaro served as moderator.

The English version presented here is by my wife, Dr. Carmen Zuk, by birth an Argentine herself, a child psychiatrist who served as my translator to the Spanish-speaking audience in Argentina. There is some amplification from the Spanish-speaking version of the summary of the case presented at the beginning, that is believed necessary to provide a sharper focus for the reader. The translation of the transcript of the discussion strives to reproduce for the English-speaking audience the closest actual intention of the speakers rather than a literal word-for-word rendering.

Case Summary

The couple in therapy is white, working class, Protestant, and in their early 30s. Neither husband nor wife completed high school. They reside at the home of the husband's mother in northeast Philadelphia. There are four children, ages four through nine. Originally the family was referred by the husband's physician because the doctor felt the husband was depressed following a third desertion by his wife. She had been living away from her family this third time for a couple of years, but her husband knew where she was living, and he would see her on the street from time to time. Therapy was not recommended for the family so long as the wife was not available, although it was suggested to the husband that he might benefit from individual therapy. About five weeks after the initial interview, he phoned the therapist to say that he had obtained the consent of his wife for couple therapy, and that she had actually returned home to live. The first interview with the couple was arranged, and three succeeding interviews were held with them. The fifth interview was recorded on film.

The Filmed Fifth Interview

The couple quickly launches into a discussion of a fight they had had the night before. They had come to blows—each had hit the other, although without serious injury. What had happened was that the day before the interview, at the suggestion of the wife, they revisited the neighborhood in which she had been living with a male friend during the period of her most recent runaway. Her explanation for this was that it would be a test of her true feelings for her husband and children. This was the way she would show her husband that her boyfriend meant nothing to her now.

The therapist says he presumes the husband responded as he did because of jealousy, and after some hesitation the husband agrees. His wife insists there was no cause for jealousy. The couple then state they are happy to be back together again, and both regret the fight.

The wife recalls that there have been previous fights, and on one occasion her husband broke several of her ribs when he threw her against a chair.

The husband complains to the therapist that his wife seldom talks to him; for instance, she doesn't talk about the interviews after leaving them even though he would like that. The wife responds that her husband can talk for hours, but always about the same things. She has heard him repeat himself so many times—just like his mother does. She doesn't want to talk much because of the presence of her mother-in-law and her children at home.

Husband and wife talk about their wish to buy a home where they could live with more privacy, but recognize it will take a long time because of lack of funds.

The wife confirms that she is pregnant. The tests were completed and the result was positive. (The therapist has been aware of this as a potentially explosive issue because almost certainly the husband was not the natural father, and he has intentionally not encouraged discussion of it.)

The husband comments that he has been working long hours at work recently, and has been tired—perhaps fatigue contributed to his loss of control yesterday. He also says he had several teeth extracted in the last couple of days, and perhaps that also contributed. The wife says with some humor that if he hits her again, she will hit him back with a frying pan, but says she is home to stay now.

The therapist intercedes strongly at that point (i.e., at her remark that she is home to stay) to comment that that is precisely what he thinks has the husband on edge, and that the visit to the neighborhood of her boyfriend was a serious threat to him. The therapist insists the husband needs reassurance that she will not run away again—and is entitled to it.

The wife becomes tearful, saying she didn't return home to "take this shit" (signifying the husband's physical abuse, perhaps also the therapist's insistence on her provocation). The therapist says she is not "a helpless little lamb." He suggests she may have needed the fight as much as her husband. The therapist says his role is as referee between the couple in incidents such as those that occurred—that's why they need him. They agree.

The Aftermath

There are five more interviews with the couple, and then termination occurred despite the therapist's suggestion of meetings about every month. The contact ended on a happy note. Husband and wife stated that there was more cooperation between them at home. They had taken the children on a few days' holiday that everyone had enjoyed just before the last interview.

About one year had passed when the therapist received a phone call from the husband telling him about events in the interim. The good relationship had continued several months. When the wife approached the term of her pregnancy, arguments again broke out. The baby was born, but lived less than 24 hours. The bickering and battling continued, and the wife decided to leave her husband again—but this time she took the children with her to the home of her mother. The husband was calling the therapist to ask him to persuade his wife to return with the children.

The therapist asked the husband to tell his wife to phone him, the therapist, which she did. She told the therapist that she wasn't ready to return to her husband. She said she was doing well with the children and needed more time. The therapist said it sounded as if she were really trying, and thanked her for phoning to let him know how she was.

Intention of Presentation

This case was not a dramatic therapeutic "cure." Rather it depicted a more or less typical outcome with a couple commonly seen in clinics or agencies handled with what is thought to be reasonable skill by the therapist. The therapist assisted in the reconciliation, and later, when serious stress again disrupted the husband-wife relationship, his efforts may have influenced the wife to evince a more mature response.

Discussion

Ms. Elzufan: I'm sorry to say I had only a quick reading of the case material and didn't see the film. I'm an exponent of the notion that nonverbal communication very much helps to understand a family. It accorded with my idea of poor neighborhoods in Philadelphia. The people look like they have lived with poverty. In general I work within the framework of short-term therapy, using short-term goals. This was a difficult and complex case in which, it seems to me, there could have been many goals for the therapist. There was a history of alcohol abuse, physical abuse, the need to overcome a special crisis in the marriage, the need to learn how to be a family. I thought about those things, and then I thought about Jay Haley who says all techniques are useful with different families. I think Dr. Zuk's results with this case are positive, while not ideal. I enjoyed in him the absence of an impression of therapist omnipotence.

Dr. Canevaro: What is your idea of the life situation of the couple—the problems they are having? How would you respond if they came to your office? What is the drama they are enacting? What would be your diagnosis?

Ms. Elzufan: I don't deal much with diagnosis. This couple is trapped in an endless game. To discover the rules of the game would make it possible to undertake a therapy that would give positive results.

Dr. Canevaro: What do you mean by "rules of the game"?

Ms. Elzufan: How they are linked to each other. Why he hits her so that she leaves, and then afterward he begs her to stay. It is a repetitive pattern in which the husband tries to solve the conflict in a way that causes the wife to repeat the sequence.

Dr. Canevaro: Does the idea of repetitive pattern explain what caused the behavior?

Ms. Elzufan: I do not think about causes so much as what purpose the behavior serves and this is difficult to pinpoint. I would do it in a more direct manner than Dr. Zuk. I would look for more concrete ways to implement a strategy, and of course that may or may not be successful. What purpose does the wife's behavior serve? Why does her husband act as he does? What are they trying to achieve through such behavior? There are gaps for me because I did not see their behavior directly on the film.

Dr. Garcia Badaracco: My first thought about this couple is that they are suffering more than they appear to be. Each one carries the weight of their personal history. I wonder about the role the therapist can play. I'm not necessarily referring to technical aspects of therapy, about which we may say more later. I am talking about the attitude of the therapist. I wonder, for instance, if I would be willing to commit the great amount of time necessary to help this couple? Would they provide me the opportunity to help them? They are a difficult couple from the standpoint of therapy. I would agree with Celia Elzufan in many of the questions she raised. They live in a country I do not know well. They have social, educational, and economic characteristics that make therapy difficult. I think I would first try to make a psychiatric diagnosis—probably describing them as acting-out personalities rather than psychopathic personalities. The alcohol addiction and certain other factors suggest a psychopathic personality structure. They are dependent on one another; the one hopes to find in the other what is missing in the self. When they fail in this, they get anxious or angry. I think the therapist would have to take charge of their immaturity and see whether they can be helped to improve their functioning. Otherwise the help available to them is limited, and I think Dr. Zuk thought so too. The therapeutic task can be seen on two levels: either the way Dr. Zuk did it or by means of a "deeper approach."

Dr. Sicardi: Well, I'm quite in agreement with what has been said so far, especially what Dr. Garcia Badracco said about the couple's suffering more than they appear to. But I would add that they also abuse each other more than they show. For instance, the wife reports a prior fight when two of her ribs were broken. I had to question the extent of a criminal motive in the husband. There was good handling by the therapist in so few interviews—especially Dr. Zuk's handling of the fight issue. There seemed to me a real catharsis when the couple could talk about such a violent episode. Change is pinpointed when the daughters sided with their mother by indicating this time they would leave with her if her husband forced her out. I do believe that one of the positive effects of the therapy was the discovery by Dr. Zuk a year after termination that the wife had left, but that this time she took her children with her to her own mother. I think it is very hard for therapists to handle violence in patients, especially if there are criminal fantasies. It is easier to handle sexual acting-out in the transference than violence, which often requires hospitalization.

Dr. Canevaro: I am not sure I understand what you mean by criminal motive. Can you explain it?

Dr. Sicardi: Well, if he could break her ribs one day, the next he could break her head.

Ms. Elzufan: With the frying pan.

Dr. Sicardi: Yes, with the frying pan.

Dr. Canevaro: I am asking about the meaning of the criminal motive. As a therapist do you ask yourself about it or let it go?

Dr. Sicardi: No, no, no. If you press me on the matter, I have to say I think there is a homosexual conflict operating in the couple. There is a reversal of their sexual roles. She is the one who leaves rather than he—usually it is the men who leave, not the women. She shames him by becoming pregnant by another man. He stays home with the children like a housewife. I have seen couples where the woman looks for a macho guy for sex, but in my judgment this is only a homosexual displacement to injure the husband. In taking her husband to the neighborhood in which she lived with her boyfriend, the wife hopes to provoke a battle between her husband and boyfriend.

Dr. Canevaro: Would you say she has a homosexual identification?

Dr. Sicardi: Yes—a frying pan has a handle, doesn't it. It is a symbol of both sexual organs, and she hit him with it.

Dr. Canevaro: You said she leaves home like men do, but have you considered the rules of their sociocultural context sufficiently? Or do you see it purely as an expression of major psychopathology?

Dr. Sicardi: Major psychopathology. Of course we could discuss the sociocultural context, but then we would be getting away from the subject, wouldn't we?

Dr. Garcia Badaracco: I think the criminal motive is very important in this case, but I wouldn't relate it to latent homosexuality. The woman may play the masculine role because she simply doesn't know what to do in this situation. There is lack of support when she needs it, and there is aggression. He doesn't know how to handle the situation either. Afterwards, he misses her and looks for her. It is really a repetition compulsion. This is a pathologic symbiotic couple with a sadomasochistic character. The homosexuality would be a mask, a screen. But I wouldn't want to introduce more psychoanalytic interpretations because I think they remove us from the main issue. Celia Elzufan spoke of uncovering the disruptive sequence of events. I don't agree with this formulation, which is a kind of interpretation, because it does not explain the difficulty the couple has in facing their conflict.

Ms. Elzufan: I was not trying to interpret the conflict; perhaps I wasn't explicit enough about that.

Dr. Garcia Badaracco: What I posit is a sadomasochistic structure where neither member of the couple can differentiate from the other, where there are constant transference reactions occurring between the two. It is necessary for the therapist to take charge of this situation which causes much suffering.

Dr. Canevaro: So your view would be that the sadomasochistic structure is primary, the homosexual conflict secondary.

Dr. Garcia Badaracco: It is a symbiotic pathologic structure which contains more psychotic than neurotic elements.

Ms. Elzufan: We seem always to end up translating the concepts of individual personality into the group and family dimension—thinking more in terms of what is happening in each individual as a separate entity rather than with the relationship itself. I would focus on the problem these people bring to the therapy. I would try to promote a change in the relationship. I would need to define the problem. If I remember correctly, they came referred by a physician— the husband first came with the children because of his depression. If this man came to me, I would ask him to explain the problem and how he has tried to solve it. I need to know what has been attempted, because people generally try many possible solutions. This is a crisis for which definite goals must be set up to promote change. If a small change can be introduced, then possibly others would occur that would be larger. I agree very much with Dr. Zuk's redefinition—the one that Alejandro referred to about the usefulness of the fight to maintain their relationship as it is. I would try to concentrate on what the Palo Alto group has called the "language" of the couple or family, their values, and ways of conducting themselves. I would take literally the fact that she runs away as a way of handling stress. I would assume she would leave again in two or three months, but in the meantime suggest to the couple that they try to enjoy this time when she has returned home, so that when she leaves again, at least they would know what it was like to have a good relationship with each other. I would take it for granted that she will leave again; moreover, I would suggest to them that they plan together her next runaway. This is a risk, but one I would be willing to take as a therapeutic maneuver.

Dr. Canevaro: This would be a kind of paradoxical intention, would it not?

Ms. Elzufan: Instead of being done in a compulsive manner, outside of their control, so to speak, the next leavetaking would be done in a planned manner. Perhaps what Dr. Zuk accomplished with the couple is the maximum that could be done, but my therapeutic strategy would be as I stated.

Dr. Sicardi: Well, I don't think I would want to force her to run away; I would try other ways. Perhaps the death of the baby precipitated her next separation. I would not want to be the one to suggest they separate. This is a very distressed couple. Perhaps the way they actually resolved the crisis is really the best that could have happened. Dr. Zuk discovered at the follow-up that the children were all right; it was said they were doing well in school. I have been thinking about what might have triggered the husband's violence. It might have been when the wife said she was going to get dinner ready. Perhaps he couldn't eat because of his bad teeth, but also I think the wife was speaking in a code. She knows there is going to be a violent fight. She knows which button to push to make the husband explode. Dr. Zuk responded in a most interesting way when he says to her in the interview that she was not an innocent lamb. I think he handled it better than I could—in a manner that produced a therapeutic catharsis. There are a number of triangular situations here: one has to do with the expected baby coming between husband and wife; another has to do with the mother-in-law coming between husband and wife. I really question whether this couple can have a marriage, and am concerned about the well-being of the children in view of the violence that characterizes the marriage. I wonder if it would not be better to see them individually. Dr. Zuk seems to suggest this at the time of follow-up when the husband calls him on the phone.

Ms. Elzufan: But at that time they were already separated, weren't they?

Dr. Sicardi: Yes, but this lady seems like a messenger dove that always comes back home. I believe I would recommend individual psychotherapy to minimize the danger of violence.

Ms. Elzufan: I would like to clarify that I didn't predict she was going to run away again. My approach was to incorporate the running away in a therapeutic strategy.

Dr. Zuk: We have had an excellent presentation in this case of two very different points of view. These are prominent in the field of family therapy today, as they have been from the beginning. I think it is important that they have been presented here in a friendly manner, because that has not always been the case. I would define Alejandro's viewpoint as psychoanalytic, and Celia's as an expression of communication theory whose main exponent is Jay Haley and the people at the Mental Research Institute in Palo Alto. Probably the psychoanalytic viewpoint dominated in the very early days of the field, but communication theory drew even in the mid 1960s. The difference between my viewpoint and psychoanalytically oriented family therapists is quite obvious, but there are also significant differences with the communicationists. My colleagues, Jorge and Alejandro, representing the psychoanalytic point of view, made reference to the couple coming from a particular social, economic, and educational class, but considered that information essentially secondary and preferred an explanation in terms of major psychopathology. My colleague Celia, representing the communicationists, also treated those facts as largely irrelevant to her conception.

Ms. Elzufan: No, I think that at the beginning. . .

Dr. Zuk: Yes, you mentioned it, but I think it had little bearing on your treatment plan. Despite the claim of the communication therapists that they consider social class and culture and the effect of crisis in formulating their therapeutic strategies, I don't see it happening. I have difficulty believing that any of my colleagues here adequately considered the cultural or educational characteristics of the couple, or the special situation where they and their children were living with a mother-in-law of the wife. I want to point out that physical abuse in their particular social class is more common than you think it would be, and should not, in and of itself, be labeled psychopathology. By comparison with the middle class, physical abuse is a much more common event in the lower socioeconomic class. If all the features of the couple are properly considered, I think that prescribing the next runaway or limiting the treatment series to, say, ten interviews would not be indicated. I agree with Alejandro that, given the couple's history, there is a high risk that she will run away again—but it is quite another thing to prescribe that she do so. What if she does it again, and when her husband asks her why, she says, because my therapist told me to? If you prescribe it, then you may be held responsible for it later in a way that you might not have originally envisioned. The therapist may have good cause to think the event will repeat, but it is rather an omnipotent attitude to insist on it. I understand it is done with a paradoxical intention, with applying a double-bind message, but it reflects a rather omnipotent attitude about human behavior—would that human behavior could be so simplified! I think it is also an oversimplification to strictly limit the contact between therapist and family—restricted to let us say eight or ten sessions. Why eight or ten; why not two or three? I hope Celia does not take this the wrong way, but I consider these issues most important.

Dr. Canevaro: Maybe what is influencing your remarks is the current condition of family therapy in the United States.

Dr. Zuk: Maybe so, but I think it is essential to point up these differences here. This discussion has been stimulating and I would like to offer a synthesis of the two points of view expressed by Jorge and Alejandro, on the one hand, and Celia on the other. Jorge and Alejandro were expressing very much what I have called "discontinuity" values; for instance, they were interested in diagnosis and prognosis, and suggested a possible referral for individual psychotherapy for treatment of major psychopathology. Celia didn't want to make a diagnosis, and would have tried to help the couple experience each other differently by directly suggesting different ways to treat each other. Jorge and Alejandro were interested in exploring the factor of hatred in the couple. Celia was interested in their more positive feelings toward each other. Celia's orientation was one that I have called "continuity" values. As a therapist with this couple, I engaged in a significant way in the role of celebrant. What is that? Well really, it was offered to me by the couple who wished to celebrate their reunion. It was important for them to have someone enact that role—it was therapeutic for them.

Dr. Canevaro: Do you think it's possible to design a therapy for families that does not take into account educational level, socioeconomic level, and the like?

Dr. Zuk: No, particularly for family therapy. Orthodox psychoanalysis, of course, was always *un*interested in these factors. Other psychoanalytic approaches have shown some mild interest; and it is my impression that in the recent interest of certain analysts in the problem of narcissism there is a significant focus on social and cultural factors. I would like to make it clear that despite differences from psychoanalysis and communication theory, I share certain elements in common with both. I also like to accent the positive whenever possible. However, I don't agree with Celia when it comes to prescribing another runaway—even if the intention in so doing is to discourage it. Families are very conservative units, thus therapists must take care lest they offer suggestions that are perceived as odd or silly or contrary to common sense. I agree with Jorge and Alejandro that there are pre-existing conditions in this couple that limit the range of treatment goals. I wouldn't strictly limit the number of treatment interviews in advance, because that seems to me an issue in which the family itself must play a larger decision-making role.

Ms. Elzufan: The communication theorists don't need me to defend them! I do think setting time limits and concrete goals increase the possibility of therapeutic success. Families like to see each interview bring them one step forward toward treatment success. I believe these techniques might help overcome the crisis with the couple, and that then a growth-oriented therapy might be possible. Incidentally, I think the idea of strictly limiting therapy to, say, ten meetings is inefficient, but ten meetings with a specific goal in mind to be met could be useful. Besides, I didn't propose that they plan her next runaway just for the purpose of paradoxical intention, but rather as a means of having them relate to each other differently. I didn't prescribe the runaway. I suggested the possibility of it in order to give them time, in the interim, to use the time they have together better. Don't I recall correctly that she ran away every three months or so? Well, then the risk of her running away again is very high; but while she is home she should try to have a positive relationship. I think the communication theorists do talk about social class, life values, and such. In the brief time I had to read the case description, I may have overlooked these things, but the communicationists don't overlook them. A main part of their work has been with lower class people—Minuchin in Philadelphia, for example.

Dr. Zuk: I can't agree. They have actually not addressed these factors.

Ms. Elzufan: I think they take them into account.

Dr. Garcia Badaracco: It's a pity we don't have more time for a deeper exchange. I believe Dr. Zuk picked up many issues, but perhaps he didn't perceive that behind those there could be deeper problems.

Dr. Zuk: Are you referring to deeper problems with the couple?

Dr. Garcia Badaracco: No. I think Dr. Zuk is too much influenced by current family therapy controversies in the United States, which don't affect us very much here. We have our own controversies in Argentina. In my work over 30 years with psychotic patients I have felt obliged to modify many aspects of psychoanalytic theory. My view of communication theory is that it is limited to certain aspects of relationships, too limited, and doesn't take into account very important dynamics. But I think there may be a way to integrate the two points of view, to overcome the apparent controversies. I got very involved in Dr. Zuk's exposition—he made a reference I found interesting. He said that Alejandro and I emphasized aggression, and concentrated on diagnostic categories—psychopathy, criminality, and so on. And he said that Celia took almost the opposite point of view. I must say I believe this is a superficial observation and shows the difficulty of a deeper exchange. I said at the beginning of our discussion that I did not know enough about the cultural background of the couple. I remarked on their aggression that indeed it could have been more a derivative of their social class than psychopathology. I believe a therapist must take factors like social class into account. It could be decisive to distinguish between whether a person has criminal potential or is merely acting within the norms of a soical class. I must say I agree to some extent with Celia's and Dr. Zuk's criticism that talking about the psychopathology of aggression might in no way have a bearing when actually doing psychotherapy with this couple.

Dr. Zuk: You were making an evaluation of each member of the couple.

Dr. Garcia Badaracco: In my style of doing therapy, I do address the positive feelings and positive changes.

Dr. Zuk: Why should those elements only be an aspect of your style? I consider that they are values expressed by the therapist and have a therapeutic role.

Dr. Garcia Badaracco: I consider the elements important in family therapy and in individual therapy as well. I am not aloof as a therapist—not a screen for the patient's projections. I offer myself as a person who can directly support the patient through the most troubled times. It is important not to interpret only in terms of negative transference or aggression or death instinct. I do not like verbal prescriptions to patients, though there may be some application for them in a limited way. I would have liked to develop an exchange with Dr. Zuk regarding the role of celebrant, because that seems to me to raise deeper issues about the psychotherapist's function. Dr. Zuk develops the concept of the celebrant—I accept it, in so far as I can understand it. The celebrant allows the couple to go through positive experiences. But that is where my doubts creep in: whether this celebrant role touches the depths of the couple's difficulties. It remains to be seen whether this pair can ever be a truly married couple. I think that to simply be a celebrant with this couple is not enough.

Dr. Zuk: It is one among three roles the therapist can use—not the only one.

Dr. Garcia Badaracco: On the whole, I would say that it was the reason why the couple discontinued treatment.

Dr. Zuk: You think the celebrant role limited therapy?

Dr. Garcia Badaracco: No, I'm not questioning the role of celebrant.

Dr. Zuk: But you think the celebrant role is a rather limited one, right?

Dr. Garcia Badaracco: I think it may well have played a role in the interruption of treatment with the couple, but this is what I would like to discuss: To what extent does the therapist have to be in charge of his patients? To give you an idea: A rather orthodox psychoanalyst believes he must interpret the material presented by the patient—to interpret the unconscious meaning. To be in charge in this instance means to evaluate and take into account the difficulty the patient may have in making use of the interpretations.

Dr. Zuk: Once you've gone that far, are you still within the psychoanalytic framework?

Dr. Garcia Badaracco: I think so. Instead of thinking that a patient is "resisting"—which is a Freudian concept—it is advantageous to think the patient is having difficulty facing certain problems in living. Incidentally, I was glad to hear Dr. Zuk mention the study of narcissism, which I consider a great step forward. But to return to the clinical case, let me say this: I believe it would not be advisable to attempt individual psychoanalysis with the couple. I would recommend couple therapy, but a deeper and wider therapy than was undertaken by Dr. Zuk, and with more time allowed.

Dr. Sicardi: I'm pretty much in agreement with what Jorge has said. Incidentally when I referred to a homosexual aspect in the couple, I didn't mean to imply that it should be interpreted to them. I also try to emphasize the positive in therapy, and I also use interpretation. I wonder if there is a possible relation between the number of the wife's pregnancies and the number of her runaways. There were four of each at the point of the last contact with her. The tenth interview with the couple has Dr. Zuk telling the couple that he would prefer to see them less frequently, but I might have liked to maintain a frequent contact to follow just how well the couple was getting along. I wouldn't have wanted either to dig things up too much, but simply to try to understand the relationship better.

Dr. Canevaro: I want to thank all of you for this productive exchange. It made me think of a parallel between family therapy and a family—both strive to develop and integrate. When a family fulfills this function, it helps to differentiate its members—allows each to become independent. Family therapy must also try to integrate its models and theories in order to fulfill its scientific function. In so doing it helps to discriminate these properly, to put them in correct perspective. Here today we have had some attempt at integration and some at differentiation, and have managed to retain mutual respect at the same time.

REFERENCES

Abraham, K. *Selected papers of Karl Abraham, M.D.* London: Hogarth Press, 1927.

Adler, A. In H.L. Ansbacher & R.R. Ansbacher (Eds.). *The individual psychology of Alfred Adler: A systematic presentation in selections from his writings.* New York: Basic Books, 1956.

Arieti, S., & Bemporad, J. The psychological organization of depression. *American Journal of Psychiatry*, 1980, *137*, 1360–1365.

Beck, A.T. Cognitive theory of depression. In P.J. Clayton & James E. Barrett (Eds.). *Treatment of depression: Old controversies and new approaches.* New York: Raven Press, 1983.

Bibring, E. Mechanisms of depression. In P. Greenacre (Ed.). *Affective disorders.* New York: International Universities Press, 1953.

Blatt, S.J. Levels of object representation in anaclitic and introjective depression. In *Psychoanalytic study of the child* (Vol. 29). New York: International Universities Press, 1974.

Bowlby, J. *Attachment.* New York: Basic Books, 1969.

Erikson, E. *Childhood and society.* New York: Norton, 1950.

Fenichel, O. *The psychoanalytic theory of neurosis.* New York: Norton, 1945.

Greenblatt, M., Becerra, R.M. & Serafetinides, E.A. Social networks and mental health: An overview. *American Journal of Psychiatry*, 1982, *139*, 977–984.

Kanner, L. Problems of nosology and psychodynamics in early infantile autism. *American Journal of Orthopsychiatry*, 1949, *19*, 416–426.

Klerman, G.L. Overview of affective disorders. In H.I. Kaplan, A.M. Freeman, & B.J. Sadock (Eds.). *Comprehensive textbook of psychiatry/III* (Vol. 2). Baltimore: Williams & Wilkins, 1980.

Lewinsohn, P. A behavioral approach to depression. In R. Friedman & M. Katz (Eds.). *The psychology of depression: Contemporary theory and research.* New York: John Wiley & Sons, 1974.

Seligman, M.E.P. *Helplessness: On depression, development, and death.* San Francisco: Freeman, 1974.

Sifneos, P.E. Brief psychotherapy and crisis intervention. In H.I. Kaplan, A.M. Freedman, & B.J. Sadock (Eds.). *Comprehensive textbook of psychiatry/III* (Vol. 2). Baltimore: Williams & Wilkins, 1980.

Spitz, R.A. Anaclitic depression. In *The psychoanalytic study of the child* (Vol. 2). New York: International Universities Press, 1946.

Stuart, R.B. *Helping couples change: A social learning approach to marital therapy.* New York: Guilford Press, 1980.

Sullivan, H.S. In H. S. Perry & M. L. Gawel (Eds.). *The interpersonal theory of psychiatry* (Vol. 1). New York: Norton, 1953.

Wolberg, L., & Aronson, M. (Eds.). *Group therapy.* New York: Intercontinental Medical Books, 1974.

Wolpert, E.A. Major affective disorders. In H.I. Kaplan, A.M. Freedman, & B.J.

Sadock (Eds.). *Comprehensive textbook of psychiatry/III*. Baltimore: Williams & Wilkins, 1980.

Zuk, G.H. On the pathology of silencing strategies. *Family Process,* 1965, *5*, 32–49.

Zuk, G.H. *Process and practice in family therapy*. Haverford, PA: Psychiatry and Behavior Science Books, 1975.

Zuk, G.H. Family therapy: Clinical hodgepodge or clinical science? *Journal of Marriage and Family Counseling*, 1976, *2*, 299–303.

Zuk, G.H. Value systems and psychopathology in family therapy. *International Journal of Family Therapy*, 1979, *1*, 133–151.

Zuk, G.H. *Family therapy: A triadic-based approach* (rev. ed.). New York: Human Sciences Press, 1981a.

Zuk, G.H. Style of relating as pathogenic relating: A family case study. *International Journal of Family Therapy*, 1981b, *3*, 16–28.

Zuk, G.H. "Ordinary People" and the truncated nuclear family. *International Journal of Family Therapy*, 1982, *4*, 23–30.

Zuk, G.H. Toward a value diffusion theory of depression. *International Journal of Family Therapy*, 1983, *5*, 155–167.

Zuk, G.H. The truncated nuclear family. *International Journal of Family Therapy*, 1985, *7*, 3–10.

INDEX